Complaining Effectively

Complain Effectively

How to by-pass Call Centres and solve your complaints

BRIAN HOMAN

BONCIL PUBLISHING

This paperback edition first published
In Great Britain in 2009 by
BONCIL PUBLISHING
4 Victory House
Higher Street
Dartmouth
Devon, TQ6 9RE

Copyright © Brian Homan 2009

Designed and illustrated by
Shaunagh Radcliffe

Printed and bound in Great Britain by
Four Way Print Limited, Unit 27A Pennygillam Way,
Pennygillam Industrial Estate, Launceston, Cornwall, PL15 7ED

The moral right of the author has been asserted.

All rights reserved. Without limiting the rights under copyright reserved above, no part of this publication may be reproduced, stored or introduced into a retrieval system, or transmitted, in any form or by any means (electronic, mechanical, photocopying, recording or otherwise), without the prior written permission of both the copyright owner and the publisher of this book.

A CIP catalogue record for this book is available from the British Library.

ISBN 978-0-9561868-0-5

Contents

Introduction	1
Are You Sitting Comfortably?	3
The Rules Of The Game	11
Banks, Bailiffs and Bother	33
A Satisfactory Result	51
Faulty Fiasco	65
Ticket To Ride	87
Staying On Track	97
Trade Secrets	105
Is This Seat Taken?	120
Bully Boys	135
The End Of The Line	152
The Rules	157

Acknowledgements

Special thanks are due to members of H.M. Police, lawyers, advice agencies and other professionals in areas including telecommunications and media studies in general, for their assistance in validating the <u>factual</u> case histories presented in this book.

A separate and very special acknowledgement is due to Shaunagh Radcliffe. Truly a remarkably talented young professional illustrator of the highest order.

Brian Homan
Dartmouth
2009

Introduction

Most of us have had occasion to complain to a company or individual about poor service, quality of goods and even alleged downright deception.

Latterly, having become convinced of the need for a guide in this thorny area, whilst helping colleagues and friends solve their own problems of this nature, I have in each instance kept notes on the progress and resolution of the issue. You can be *certain* that every case history in this book is based on real people and *factual* evidence.

To Complain Effectively, discipline and control will be your watchwords; dealing with the opposition requires a firm calm rein on your emotions. Lose your cool and you'll lose objective commonsense. To win, outbursts of indignation – however justified you may feel in giving vent to them – *must* be resisted. Ice cold all the time please.

The purpose of this book is to guide you step by step to a satisfactory resolution of your problem; in the process it is designed to enable you to free yourself from stress and anger.

A cautionary note: the opposition may be extremely bright. Don't try to be clever, remain patient and persistent. Please ensure you keep to the solid proven techniques demonstrated, they will not let you down; just follow the rules.

It may be that all you require is a courteous apology, the refund of monies owed or possibly you seek damages for stress and harassment. I cannot provide a panacea, I *can* equip you with the means to achieve a satisfactory solution.

Brian Homan

CHAPTER 1

Are you sitting comfortably?....

CHAPTER 1

COOL DOWN AND ASSESS THE SITUATION

Sit, down, preferably in a room where you will not be disturbed. You will need a clear table or desk, a pen and a note-pad and, of course, all the correspondence relating to your complaint, whether in the form of letters, e-mail or faxes. Sort all correspondence in date order and keep it in one pile with the earliest communication on top. I assume, at this stage, that you *have* correspondence: if not, or have not as yet made any complaint, this will be covered in due course. If possible, have beside you copies of your detailed phone bills, again in date order, earliest on top.

Now try to remember as far as possible any telephone calls you have made or received which relate in any way to your complaint. Make separate notes of these, detailing, again as far as possible, what was said during each call. Include approximate dates and times. At all costs, don't panic if you are unable to remember anything! Relax. Inevitably, while you have been attempting to recall these details you will begin to feel emotionally involved. The moment you become aware of this, however, is the moment you are back in control. You will soon realise that the calmer you are the sooner you will be able to think clearly. Now you have sorted out your papers and made some notes, we can begin the next stage.

ADDRESSING THE SITUATION

To decide on *our* strategy and tactics, documentary evidence is needed in support of *your* case, if any such evidence exists.

It is at this stage that *you* must ask yourself some serious questions. The answers *you* give yourself determine whether in all honesty and good conscience you should proceed with the complaint.

When you answer these questions, ask yourself 'what evidence in written form do I have to support my case?' Don't worry if you do not, in fact, have any hard evidence at this stage. The objectivity and honesty you apply to your answers will decide for you whether you go ahead or not.

Ask yourself:
1. Will a simple apology from the company suffice?
2. Do I want an apology plus a refund of money and expenses incurred?
3. Do I feel that over and above 1 and 2 I insist the company pays me a sum to cover the stress and time involved ('damages') in my claim against them?

Consider all three points and put your claim in the appropriate category.

Now comes the difficult bit: keep calm and evaluate honestly whether the facts you are able to marshal *genuinely support your claim*.

If, after careful consideration they do not obviously support your claim, swallow your pride and anger and put the whole thing down to experience. Where is the point in pursuing the matter if you know in your heart of hearts you have no case? The company will know it if you do.

Before *we* get into the 'how' of making an effective complaint it is important to look further into the considerations involved in deciding whether a complaint is justified in the first place. If it is, *we* shall need to decide when to start the complaint procedure.

All too often, in the heat of the moment, we are inclined to pick up the telephone or blast off a letter, e-mail or fax loaded with abuse without giving the recipient of the tirade any chance to be helpful or even to get a word in edgeways.

For instance: a customer makes a purchase from a retail shop. Let us assume it is a last minute birthday gift for a child. The gift is a beautifully packaged doll. You are scarcely likely to rip off the packaging in the shop to check that the doll is faultless. It is also reasonable to assume you will not be tearing off the packaging at home to inspect the doll before sending if off in the post and even less likely if you intend to deliver it by hand.

The package is received by the child who is devastated to discover that the doll's head falls off as the gift is unwrapped. Of course you are going to complain!

Let us leave this example aside for a moment. Now for another. (Be patient. You will shortly understand the reason for these examples). A customer goes to a greengrocer and buys a large green pepper. This customer is unlikely to produce a knife in the shop and cut the pepper in half simply to confirm there is nothing unpleasant inside. (I assume for the sake of argument that the pepper is not encased in a plastic bubble). The vegetable is subsequently prepared at home by the customer who discovers a large white slug-like creature alive inside. You may have guessed that I speak from personal experience! Here is another example where there are legitimate grounds for complaint.

Now it could be that the doll was purchased in a town 40 miles distant from where the purchaser lives, whilst the pepper was bought just across the road from home. Evidently the restitution/compensation in the two examples will follow a different pattern – in the first case, it may be necessary to telephone the shop, explain the problem and ask how to proceed. In the second instance, I called at the greengrocer's, showed him the evidence, received a profuse apology and an invitation to help myself to produce free of charge.

These two example illustrate (only) a minute sampling of the enormous range of individual complaints generated daily. They should also stimulate the process of considering the many ways open to you in your quest for a satisfactory outcome to your own complaint.

It will immediately be apparent that picking up the telephone and screaming out your frustration is scarcely likely to gain a sympathetic hearing.
Different types of complaint need different handling, so much is patently obvious. However, at the risk of repeating myself ad nauseam, here comes one more example: Imagine a situation where you have paid a deposit on a particular item. You fail to receive it. Even a courteous telephone call proves fruitless; you are unlikely to get your money back, especially if you were promised delivery on a specific day and time. It is now two weeks late and you have already been fobbed off with excuses, having made half a dozen telephone calls.

The lesson to be learnt here is that you should never part with your money until the goods or services have been satisfactorily delivered. Individual proprietors, or 'one man bands' are often the villains in this area, likely to abscond or set up in business under a different name if you pursue them for a substantial sum. Even if only a small sum is involved, do you really want the inconvenience and unpleasantness involved in pursuing them in the Small Claims Court? Even if you win your claim, there is no guarantee that they will pay up. Be warned!

The aim of this book is explicitly to equip you properly to fight a justifiable claim successfully against an unfair, unscrupulous, unreasonable company or individual who may well lie or cheat to get out of their obligation to you.

In the pages that follow, you will be shown the strict discipline and techniques required to help you to win, but it cannot be over-emphasised that you must *stick absolutely to the rules*. At times it will be vital to go into great detail and you may sometimes feel that I am overstating the obvious. Remember that there will be some readers perhaps too young and inexperienced or too old and infirm to know how to compose an appropriate letter, let alone to be able to put together a reasoned and possibly detailed letter of complaint. *Don't worry*! There are numerous example letters in this book to show you how.

My endeavour is to help as many age groups and ability ranges as possible.

To conclude this chapter I now list the basic categories of complaint with which we shall be dealing in depth.

BASIC TYPES OF COMPLAINT

a) A person borrows money intending to repay it with interest over a given period of time; however, due to unforeseen circumstances they fail to complete the repayments. This category will not cover help to people who borrow money knowing full well they have no intention of repaying it.

b) Goods and/or services purchased on a credit contract where such goods/services prove to be either non-existent or unsatisfactory. The seller may refuse to refund a deposit and insist on receiving the full balance of payment.

c) A purchaser sends money for goods that fail to arrive, or a service that does not materialise.

d) A purchaser sends money for goods/services which turn out to be shoddy.

There are of course innumerable variations and sub-categories of these basic problems. Once you have grasped the principles – the rest will be straightforward.

Follow the rules step by step where they apply in whichever category: deviation may well create an unforeseen element of risk to your argument. It is important not to provide the opposition with extra ammunition.

Finally, may I recommend, with a gentle smile, that when you have won your battle you do not exploit the advantage. Know when to settle a dispute and draw the proverbial line under the matter.

CHAPTER 2

The Rules of the Game

CHAPTER 2

This chapter sets out a number of rules involved in following an actual case history from start to finish. The names of individuals and companies have been deleted or disguised to preserve anonymity.

Mrs T is an elderly lady in poor health suffering from severe arthritis and increasing bouts of memory loss. She lives alone in long-term rented accommodation consisting of a small ground floor flat. She has few surviving relatives who are elderly like herself and live several hundred miles away. Proud and independent-minded, she came to me for help.

Having exhausted her few savings, Mrs T lives quietly and prides herself on her ability to manage her own affairs.

She explained to me that one day she 'saw salvation' (!) in the form of a letter she received in the post originating from a well-known commercial bank. Their loans department was making an offer of money lent at an interest payable over a given period. Having told no one of this offer she made calculations based on her pension income and concluded she would be able to afford the repayments. She therefore accepted what she thought was the bank's 'kind offer'.

Amazingly, having told no one of this she managed to repay all the loan over a two year period.

Finally, she came to me with an armful of correspondence from the bank and told me the whole story. The loan had been spent on essential expenses which, although she did not know this at the time, would have been provided free of charge by the state. At first proud of her achievement, she was puzzled, then alarmed to receive letters and statements from the bank demanding further payments. By now utterly confused and desperately worried; since the letters had been accompanied by numerous telephone calls from bank employees about regular 'penalty' sums for non-payment added to each succeeding statement, she sought my help as a friend of many years.

On agreeing to help her, I first of all put her request to act for her in this dispute on a formal basis. A written agreement, witnessed by a solicitor, made it abundantly clear that I would not accept any payment or gift in kind, at any time now or in the future, for undertaking the affair and giving it my best efforts. This essential precaution protected me as well as Mrs T within a legally correct framework. I immediately informed the commercial bank of this arrangement.

My next task was to put the whole of Mrs T's correspondence with the bank in date order; a task which involved concentrated reading and note-taking and took the best part of two days to complete. Only then did I feel that I was fully acquainted with the situation.

At this stage I became convinced that something was missing from the bank's calculations. I felt equally convinced that something had been added to them. Mrs T had kept meticulous accounts and records as far as I was able to judge but her record of events definitely did not agree with what the bank was claiming. At this point I would ask you to observe how the RULES to which vital adherence must be maintained, are applied in the case of Mrs T's dispute with the bank.

THE RULES IN PRACTICE

These must be adhered to at all times and without exception.

RULE 1

THE TELEPHONE; MOBILES INCLUDED:

When the telephone rings, give your name only. Listen, but say nothing if it is the bank. When the caller has had his or her say, ask for their full name, then replace the receiver.

Upon replacing the receiver after a 'bank' call, immediately make a note on your pad of the caller's name; the time and date of the call and of course the 'gist' of what he or she had to say.

Keep the telephone notes in date order for future reference.

Put an aide-memoir on the telephone to remind you to stick rigidly to this discipline.

E-MAILS AND FAXES:

At this stage do not even think of responding. Read them and keep them on file *in date order.*

LETTERS

Under no circumstances should you respond at this stage.

RULE 2

COMMUNICATING WITH THE BANK:

NEVER, under any circumstances, TELEPHONE the bank!

All our rules are essential; this one is sovereign.

A single example of the consequence of breaking this rule will illustrate its importance. In all probability the number given on the bank's stationery as a 'help line' will in fact be their 'Dedicated Call Centre'.

If you disregard this rule, your call will cost you a lot of money. Even if the prefix to the number shown is 0800 (free call) do not telephone. *Any* other prefix to the number will *certainly* cost you money.

Apart from the potential cost of the call, the tedium and delays inherent in wading through a menu of options (even if you reach a person you think is going to help you) you will inevitably hear the anonymous voice telling you that the call 'may be monitored for training purposes'.

Should you unwisely disregard my advice and continue, you have fallen victim to a technique designed to free the real managers of a business from being side-tracked, instead of getting on with their job of empire building. You, on the other hand, are being side-tracked into involvement with their own complaints procedure. You will be led down blind alleys, huge time-lags will be created, with evasion after evasion, causing you further anxiety and, they hope, forcing you in the end to give up. As a last resort, you may be told you can obtain the services of an 'Ombudsman' or some other 'independent' body to look into your complaint.

Should you actually persevere to this stage, do you honestly believe that this so-called independent adjudicator is really going to spend hours – days, even – going through all your papers, relevant verbal background information, etc? Would anyone go to all this trouble just for you? Think again.

Do not pick up that telephone. You are likely to say something which may be used against you as long as your case is under consideration.

To sum up the position as we stand; it should be quite clear to you now that we have closed down our communication with the bank and are refusing to contact them despite their threats masquerading as requests.

Having achieved this, it is now time to prepare our first attack. We are going to write our first letter to the bank. This will require some preparatory work, so here comes the next RULE.

RULE 3

ONLY WRITE DIRECTLY TO THE CHAIRMAN OF THE COMPANY.

Sometimes, though rarely, the Top Person in an organisation may be the Managing Director or C.E.O. (Chief Executive Officer) but whatever the case may be, we must discover that person's correct title and full name. To write to, for instance, 'The Chairman' is not enough. You must address yourself to a name and title of office.

To find this information, we use one or all of a number of methods.

a) If we are dealing with an important organisation, a visit (not a telephone call) to the local library will usually get results. If you are unfamiliar with the relevant reference books or are unable to use a computer, no matter. Library staff are always glad to help. They will often provide you with the name and title of the person you need to contact by checking their computer but at the very least they will find you a telephone number.

b) If you have nothing more than a telephone number, this is one of the *very rare* occasions when you must break the rule not to telephone. The information you seek, i.e. the top person's name and title, is essential to your strategy.

c) Having dialled the number, you will usually get through to the General Enquiries desk. Confine yourself to giving your name and ask to be put through to the Chairman's office. When you are put through, ask firmly and politely 'who is speaking, please?' If the answer is 'Jean' or 'Miss Callan', ask for the person's full name. Explain that you are writing to the Chairman and would like that person's full name plus the correct postal address. You may expect to be given this information straight away but you may sometimes be asked initially 'can I help you in any way?' in which case you politely decline help, pointing out courteously that you will be making a private written complaint strictly for the attention of the Chairman and that it is an extremely delicate and personal matter. This should certainly get you the information you require and at the same time prevent the person you are speaking to from suggesting that he or she should put you through to the Call Centre Help Line.

d) An alternative method would be to telephone the advertising department for the name and official title of the Chairman. They would doubtless be sufficiently nonplussed to give you the information. You will possibly think of other ways of eliciting the facts; I myself have never had a problem in obtaining them from the Chairman's PA.

We are now ready to write that all important first letter to the bank. We have the Chairman's name and the correct postal address (Head Office) where he conducts his business; the real decision maker is in our sights, which leads us to our next rule.

RULE 4

RECORDED DELIVERY

EVERY LETTER YOU WRITE TO THE BANK MUST BE SENT BY THIS METHOD.

Photocopy the original letter you send by recorded delivery and staple the Post Office receipt to your photocopy; file it.

I emphasise these simple procedures because all too often, I have seen originals filed and the photocopy sent to the addressee. Make sure you staple that receipt of posting to your letter; paper clips are unreliable little beasts and you could end up with a pile of Post Office receipts detached from their copy letters. The resultant time-wasting re-sorting of letters and receipts should be avoided at all costs; I speak from experience.

Why Recorded Delivery? Because it ensures that when you write a letter it must be signed for on receipt by the addressee, in this case, the bank. The person who signs for it does so on a pad retained by the delivering post-person. If the sender feels it is necessary to have proof of delivery the Royal Mail will provide a copy of the validation receipt with signature.
Royal Mail also offers a 'super fast' *overnight recorded delivery* service which guarantees next day delivery. Both RECORDED and GUARANTEED deliveries require a signature of receipt and acceptance. The main difference for our purposes between the two services is that GUARANTEED delivery is quicker. Usually, I use simple Recorded Delivery as it is sufficient (for our purposes) and a lot cheaper.

For our present requirements we need to pre-empt any excuse by the bank that Mrs T's first letter – and any subsequent ones, have been mislaid, not delivered, cannot be found or worst of all, been received but completely ignored. I have ample evidence to show that major companies as well as smaller fry resort to such ruses to confuse the issue. In particular, the non-response ploy is used to persuade a customer to telephone. In the case of Mrs T it was very clear why the bank wanted her to do that.

It might be necessary to send another letter by Recorded Delivery if the non-response tactics are resorted to; more of that in our next chapter.

Be assured that the attention, down to the smallest detail, lavished on our first letter will not be lost on the Chairman, who will begin to experience the first stirrings of disquiet. He will have realised already that there is a possibility the irritating Mrs T will not so easily be put off.

These preparations completed, it is time to sit down in a calm, confident state of mind to compose our first letter. Have several sheets of A4 (I prefer *unlined*) paper to hand. Take up your pen or type if you prefer. You may have to write it out more than once before it looks 'professional'. Make sure it is legible!

Now follows the first letter from Mrs T to the bank:

RECORDED DELIVERY

Mrs Annabella R. Turkin
116G Floxam Villas
Ballinty Avenue
Sleginhope, RX9 400
(date)
My Ref. L/1/AT

Mr A, Bloggin, Chairman
-     Bank plc
Head Office
(address)

Dear Mr Bloggin,

    Re my account number (-------) LOAN ACCOUNT

    I enclose herewith copies of all correspondence received from your company concerning my account with the bank, i.e. letters dated (-------). These are for your perusal.

    I am thoroughly dissatisfied with the manner in which your company is conducting this matter. In addition I take great exception to the frequent telephone calls made to my home number by members of your staff.

    These letters and calls are seriously affecting my health.

    Kindly send me a copy of the agreement you allege I have made with the bank so that I may re-examine the situation.

    I am in no doubt that I have repaid in full the amount due to your organisation.

    Yours sincerely,
    (signature)

Copies, as appropriate

Notes on the contents of this first letter to the bank:

By enclosing copies of *all* letters received from the bank and listing their dates in the text, Mrs T has acknowledged receipt of them; she had failed to do this before. She has now implied by asking for a copy of the alleged 'agreement' that she intends to get to grips with the problem.

In fact, Mrs T could not remember actually signing *any* agreement. She even told me she was 'pretty sure' she had done no such thing. All she could remember was some sort of form asking for her details, which she completed and returned. What a pity she had not made a copy of this form at the outset! Mrs T was adamant that the form was 'not a contract'.

Note that I have not specifically forbidden the bank to telephone (See comments on Using the Telephone earlier in this chapter).

The 'copies as appropriate' at the foot of the letter refer to Mrs T's own file copy but the bank does not know that.

THE ENVELOPE

BY RECORDED DELIVERY

    For the personal attention of:
    Mr A, Bloggin, Chairman
    ----- Bank plc
    Head Office
    (address)

PRINT YOUR OWN NAME AND ADDRESS ON THE BACK OF THE ENVELOPE.

Now take your letter in its sealed envelope to the Post Office and ask the clerk to send it by RECORDED DELIVERY. Keep the receipt in a safe place until you arrive home and file it with the copy of your letter.

It is a good idea to ask also for a separate receipt for the cost of sending the letter, which should be kept in the log of expenses incurred in your dealings with the bank.

The example of Mrs T's first letter shows how to put the complainant in the driving seat, as it were. You have now set certain GUIDELINES, in particular that the only two-way communication left open to the opposition is *by letter*. We have established that your telephone is a one-way ('them to you') line of communication.

They can talk to you as much and as often as they like on the telephone. You will listen, but not comment on what they say. Actually explain this to the caller.

The only way they will ever obtain a reply from you is by Recorded Delivery letter. So if they don't write, neither will you … or will you?

In the following section, you will see how we give the bank a specific time to answer this first letter. If a reply is received within the time limit we set, all well and good. If not, all is *still* well and good! As you will see…..

For simplicity's sake, and also for a very good reason, I shall call the date on which Mrs T posts her letter 'Day Zero'. This is because I have put a maximum time limit of zero + eight days to allow for a reply.

You may well say: 'Why not wait for a while, then if no reply is received after, say, zero + thirty days, it may mean that the bank have decided to drop the whole thing?' Unfortunately, there is no possibility of this happening. The bank's aim is to squeeze more money out of Mrs T.

You may also think I am being unrealistic in setting a limit of zero + eight days; such a short period, you may say, is unreasonable. You are right!

The Chairman is highly likely to send a memo to relevant staff instructing them to send him a report on Mrs T's loan account. He will then almost certainly have another stab at distancing himself from the matter by getting a more senior member of staff to write to Mrs T.

Indeed, this is exactly what he does. Mrs T receives a letter from the bank just within her time limit. I quote:

PO Box -----
Ref Code (---)

Dear ------

Re ------

Thank you for you recent correspondence regarding your account.

We acknowledge your comments and have noted your points carefully. As such, we are collating all the relevant information from the departments that have been dealing with your account. This will allow us to investigate your query fully and enable a full response to be issued shortly.

We appreciate that you would like this matter resolved as soon as possible and so have put in place internal procedures for handling complaints fairly and speedily. These include set times for acknowledging and responding to you. In this respect we aim to achieve the following service standards:

Acknowledge all written complaints within 48 hours.
Action and/or return 90% of customer complaint phone calls the same day with the rest within 24 hours latest.
Any customer complaint by telephone not resolved by close of business the next working day will also receive a written acknowledgement.
Action Data Protection and Credit Bureau requests within 5 working days.

In the meantime if you have any concerns please do not hesitate to contact us on (number) 0870 ----

Yours sincerely,
(signature)

Operations Administration

ANALYSIS OF CONTENT

a) This letter is clearly not signed by the Chairman. Whether or not he has actually read Mrs T's letter is of no consequence at this stage.

b) The bank's headed notepaper does not give the Chairman's Head Office address, only an anonymous PO Box number.

c) The letter originates from the bank's Operations Administration Department and is signed with an unclear signature with no printed name or position.

d) With or without instructions from the Chairman, the writer of the letter ignores or pretends not to realise what is happening. Saying 'they will respond shortly' does not cover the fact that they have failed to send a copy of the alleged agreement.

e) By listing all the 'excellent' mechanisms they have put in place to achieve their service standards, they imply your problem will be solved if you slot into their 'procedure system'. (This is what Mrs T is not going to do).

f) They would like Mrs T to telephone them. They would, wouldn't they? Note the number they give with the 0870 prefix! A call to this number will cost you the proverbial 'arm and leg'. It is, of course, the number of the company's own Dedicated Call Centre.

To summarise the underlying implications of this letter:

In their eyes, Mrs T is just another upset customer whose first letter to the Chairman will be downgraded to the level of the bank's stylized complaints system. The company has constructed and implemented a system whereby nothing so mundane as a complaint is allowed to reach the Chairman.

Of course, if the organisation were doing a good job to ensure customer satisfaction they would not need a hugely expensive Call Centre and complex lengthy complaints procedures. It is likely they are failing to satisfy a substantial number of customers.

WHAT TO DO NEXT?

Check the date of the bank's letter (not the date of its arrival) and mark the day on your calendar for zero + twelve: 'letter received from the bank yet?'

RULE 5

KEEP A CALENDAR SOLELY AND SPECIFICALLY FOR 'COMPLAINTS'

You never know, but let us hope you will not have to complain about anything else in the near future. This is, in any case, an essential discipline, vital in the current

instance. You will notice that our 'response delay' period is shortening; zero + twelve days is only four days after Mrs T received her letter from the bank's Operations Administration Department.
It is indeed only a short time, deliberately so. We are now about to perform a little blood-letting operation on our distant and recalcitrant Chairman. Further treatment will come his way before long, until such time as he capitulates, responds directly to Mrs T and shows a reasonable attitude. He will, but there is some way still to go.

During the four day waiting period, you will be preparing your Second Letter to the Chairman on behalf of Mrs T. You will need this period of preparatory time not just because of the complexity of the letter but because of the sheer determination, perseverance and attention to detail required of you.

SECOND LETTER:

RECORDED DELIVERY

> Your name and address as before
> (date)

Chairman's name and address as before

Dear Chairman, (note the new formality)

    Further to my letter dated (....) and sent Recorded Delivery which included copies of earlier correspondence from your bank relating to the dispute in hand, please find enclosed once again, copies of all relevant correspondence plus a copy of my original covering letter.

    In addition, I also enclose a copy of a letter dated (....) from one of your subordinate members of staff, apparently in your Operations Administration Department. This letter indicates that the department has either taken upon itself the task of solving my problem with your bank or has received instructions to do so.

    I can only conclude that my earlier Recorded Delivery letter addressed specifically to you for your personal attention was not received by your good self. If this is the case, I am happy to take up the matter with the Royal Mail to verify the 'receipt of delivery' signature. Perhaps in the meantime you will investigate whether the envelope with my letter and copies of correspondence was signed for without your knowledge, the contents examined by a member of staff and actioned without reference to you. If this is the case, you will no doubt take appropriate action. Please let me know.

    The possibility that the most senior member of a major company should show a lack of courtesy in failing to provide a customer with a personally written response to a letter directly addressed to that person is of course unthinkable.

    Yours faithfully,
    (signature)

Copies: Operations Administration
              And as appropriate.

We have not yet quite finished with this stage of our attack.

In a suitable envelope, place the original of this letter together with all copies of other letters as indicated. Take to the Post Office for Recorded Delivery. Make sure that all details of address (your own included) are reproduced on the envelope as before in your first letter. Be certain to attach a copy of the Recorded Delivery receipt to the copy of the letter now being sent. Don't forget to file all documents, including the cash receipt, in their appropriate place.

As you already have on file photocopies of the copy letters included with your second letter, no more are required; your file retains the master photocopy set.

LETTER TO THE OPERATIONS ADMINISTRATION DEPARTMENT

No recorded delivery is required for the envelope containing a *photocopy* of this letter to the Chairman, nor do you require to enclose copies of the correspondence sent to the Chairman. It is not the business of the Operations Administration Department. Don't forget to tick 'copies' – this is to indicate it is just for their information, but in any case mark the letter 'For Information Only'.

To sum up what this letter to the Chairman is intended to achieve:

a) It shows plainly that any letter from the bank will simply result in a direct response *to the Chairman*. This saps morale.

b) The writer, Mrs T, is forcing the bank to realise she expects special treatment and refuses to be squeezed into the bank's sausage machine.

The principles, techniques and disciplines I have outlined in logical sequence will apply to your own *Complain Effectively* endeavours, just as successfully as they have done in Mrs T's case.

There is, of course, still some way to go before we reach our objective.

CHAPTER 3

Banks, Bailiffs and Bother

CHAPTER 3

To date, we are doing well, sticking to our rules. We are dealing calmly and sensibly with each new exigency as it arises. We shall continue to do so, examining every new twist and turn with full attention to detail and implications.

Now we allow two weeks to elapse, awaiting a reply to our second Recorded Delivery letter addressed to the Chairman of the Commercial Bank for his personal attention. It is important to keep in the back of your mind the fact that this bank, based in the U.K. is only a small subsidiary of the global corporation with headquarters in the USA. Putting this into perspective, the U.K. Chairman may well be 'cock of the roost' as far as his own staff are concerned, but in the overall picture he is merely a cog in the wheel. A fairly important cog, perhaps, but compared with the real masters, the President and International Group Main Board, he is only a member of staff. He can be sacked.

With this in mind, we shall communicate with the Bank only when we deem it appropriate and always, of course, by Recorded Delivery letter.

Reader, we are continuing to build an impenetrable wall of silence, to be broken only at our choosing. The Chairman is doing his best to regain control over Mrs T, trying to enforce his own policy. To date he is failing miserably. His attempt to erect his own wall of silence by distancing himself from the dispute and using his staff to communicate with Mrs T is failing signally to elicit a response from us.

He must initiate some method of opening up a dialogue: action in one form or another will be necessary in order to progress the Bank's alleged claims.

It is a certainty that someone will eventually write to Mrs T. Meanwhile, the lady has continued to received regular statements of account, each one illustrating mounting sums of money allegedly overdue. These statements are meaningless because they are non-productive for the Bank.

If the Bank is to get anywhere with Mrs T it has only one option: to send her a letter indicating new information which will prompt us to reply.

Time passes. It is now six weeks since we have received anything of substance. At last, Mrs T receives the following letter:

PO Box ------
Ref Code (---)
(Date)

Dear Mrs T

Account Number ----

    Thank you for you recent correspondence regarding your account.
    We would like to inform you that we have sent a copy of your original application form which will reach you shortly.
    Should you require any further assistance, please do not hesitate to contact our Customer Services Department on 0870 ----

Yours sincerely,

Operations Administration

* Please quote your – digit account number on all correspondence.

ANALYSIS OF THIS LETTER

a) We note the usual PO Box number as a substitute for the Bank's full address. Clearly the intention is to persuade Mrs T to telephone the Help Line, in other words, the Call Centre or rather the 'sausage machine' which costs the customer money to ring.

b) The writer *claims* to be forwarding a copy of an alleged application form, adding that 'it will reach you shortly'.

Of course, if they really had such a document it would radically affect the *terms* of the dispute: to be of any value, this alleged copy would need to be completed by or on behalf of Mrs T. Not being completed and/or signed by her, it would have no legal standing unless the person signing for it had official authorisation to do so. However, as I have emphasised at the beginning of this saga, I trust Mrs T implicitly so I intend to ignore this letter and await the document the Bank claims to be sending.

Some considerable time passes. There is no sign of this alleged 'copy'. Reader, it never, to this day, arrived! Nor indeed did the Bank ever subsequently claim that it was sent.

It is reasonable to suppose that if an original signed application form had indeed been in the Bank's possession at the outset of the dispute, a copy would have been dispatched promptly to Mrs T.

We shall certainly not forget the Bank's apparently bare-faced falsehood in this connection, intended, at the very least, to manoeuvre Mrs T into an untenable position.

We will make use of this ploy at a later date to bedevil the Bank in subsequent correspondence *if necessary*.

We continue to maintain our own splendidly aloof silence as still more time passes and we await the arrival of the non-existent 'application form'.

Clearly, we have won a valuable point, but at this stage we are not in a position to feel more than a sense of satisfaction. Something must surely be afoot in the enemy camp…

With the inevitability of winter following summer, a letter arrives from a Debt Collection Agency! Yes, here come those dreaded bailiffs!

Let us read the letter before analysing its content:

Telephone -----
Fax -----
Our Reference -----
(Date)

Dear Mrs T,

Client -----
Account -----
Balance Outstanding -----

This debt has been assigned to --------------. It is essential all future payments are made direct to -----------.

You must let us have your immediate proposals for payment of the outstanding balance by calling ---------- within 48 hours.

Alternatively, you can complete and return the insertion, headed 'payment options' by return enclosing your first payment. A pre-paid envelope has been provided for your convenience.

Payment proposals may be accepted or rejected at our discretion.

Yours sincerely,

Team Leader

ANALYSIS OF THIS LETTER

a) We learn that the alleged debt (now the principle outstanding balance plus a huge sum claimed in interest) has been 'assigned' or 'passed on to' the writers of the letter, a Debt Collection Agency *instructed by one of the Bank's associate companies.*

b) It is clear the Debt Collection Agency has been informed it can take an agreed fee/commission if it obtains the money. This operates on the basis that the Agency takes the money directly from the customer and then, but only then, deducts its fee and passes on the residue to the client, in this case, the associate company of the Bank. Thus, the implication is that the associate company then takes its own cut of the cake. Eventually, the Bank receives what is left. If everything goes according to plan, all those concerned make money out of Mrs T.

c) Note the use of 'must', 'immediate', '48 hours' and 'may be accepted or rejected'. This is a prime example of the 'bully boys' technique.

I need hardly add that we maintain *total silence*.

I next apprise Mrs T of the letter and ask her to request the identity of any caller or callers at her home by putting their ID card through the letterbox for perusal. If she does not wish to open the door or even to talk to them whilst they stand outside with the door shut, she is perfectly entitled to tell them to go away. Under no circumstances should she admit them to her house. My concern is that bailiffs from the Debt Collection Agency may call. I would add that if they were foolish enough to attempt a forced entry without legal authority, Mrs T would be seriously upset. It is very important that I minimise as far as possible, any stress on Mrs T.

In my experience, Debt Collection Agencies of repute (and there *are* a few), would *never* act outside the law. They need to go through a series of correct procedures before ever reaching the stage of entering a property illegally. In any case, Mrs T tells me she is not in the least perturbed at the thought (mmm…). She *says* she is quite content to telephone me if anything untoward occurs. She is on safe ground – nothing untoward ever does occur to trouble her as you, reader, will see as we progress.

And now, dear reader, relax and take a deep breath: this letter is just another 'try on' as you will discover.

Nine days go by (to answer your unspoken question). Have patience!

Now here we go again: another letter arrives, this time from the solicitors *acting on behalf of the Associate Company acting for the Bank*. Note, as you re-read this sentence, the labyrinthine machinations of the Bank!

I now quote the letter from the solicitors:

(Date)

Dear Mrs T,

Creditor -----
Reference No. -----
Balance Overdue -----

We have been instructed to issue legal proceedings against you for the above overdue amount unless payment in full is made immediately.

Payments, correspondence, queries and telephone calls in response to this letter must be directed to the CREDITOR'S MANAGING AGENTS, Messrs -------, telephone number 0870 etc.

If you do not make payment or reach an agreement within 5 days a Court Claim may be issued.

ANALYSIS OF THIS LETTER

The above letter arrived through Mrs T's letter box hot on the heels of the letter from the Debt Collection Agency.

These solicitors, you will note, have been appointed by the Commercial Bank's Associate Company. They state:

a) They are going to issue legal proceedings against Mrs T unless payment in full is made immediately. As I mentioned before, you will now see that they are aboard the anticipated 'gravy train', their angle being to process court proceedings against Mrs T.

   To be clear, the Associate Company – tied to the Commercial Bank – is now designated 'creditor' and the 'managing agents' are the Debt Collection Agency to whom 'all monies' (leached from Mrs T) 'must be paid'. All this is about as important as watching paint dry, in terms of what action we shall be taking. It is, nevertheless, a useful example for you in terms of how these wretched creatures operate.

b) The message they convey is the threat that unless Mrs T pays up in full or reaches an agreement with the Debt Collection Agency to pay instalments within five days, she *may* be issued with a court claim.

Immediately after the fore-going letter from the solicitors, the Debt Collection Agency chips in with another letter to Mrs T:

Telephone -----
Fax -----
(Date)

Dear Mrs T,

Our Clients -----
Reference No. -----
Balance Outstanding -----

You have failed to respond to our previous communication therefore an agent may now be instructed to call at your address to collect the amount owed to our client, or attempt to arrange suitable payment terms.

To prevent this, you must telephone one of negotiators within the next 72 hours.

Yours sincerely,

Collections Executive.

ANALYSIS OF THIS LETTER

a) Note the use of the word 'may' in the first sentence, also 'call at your address'.

b) In the second sentence, the use of 'must telephone' and 'within the next 72 hours'.

They are obviously intent on 'putting the frighteners' on our Mrs T.

I discuss these letters with Mrs T and she affirms my strong recommendation to remain silent.

You, reader, will see why in due course.

Within three days of receipt of the above two letters, a third follows, addressed to me personally for the first time. This is from the Debt Collection Agency:

Telephone -----

Professor Brian Homan
(Date)
Address

Dear Professor Homan,

Your Client: Mrs T
Our Client -----
Client Reference -----
Balance outstanding -----

    Thank you for your recent letter the contents of which have been noted. Having investigated your client's dispute we can inform you that the agreement your client would have had with (the Bank) would have been a signed agreement for a credit card.
    (Name of Bank) would not have released any funds without the agreement being signed.
    I appreciate that your client claims to have borrowed only £--- and has paid this back, but the agreement would have clearly stated what other charges she would have been liable for if the account was not cleared on a monthly basis.
    Further to the concerns that our company has now been passed (about) your client's account, this is due to the fact that there have been no payments on the account since ---- and your client has failed to come to an arrangement with us. She would have had monthly statements and letters advising her of the consequences of non-payment.
    Please can you now forward your client's proposal to clear the balance outstanding as a matter of urgency. I appreciate that your client is an elderly lady and on limited income but I can look at a payment plan to accommodate her situation.

Yours sincerely,

Team Leader

ANALYSIS OF THE LETTER

It has at last sunk into their heads that it is pointless to write to Mrs T.

It should also be equally clear to them that sending the bailiffs round to call on Mrs T would be a fruitless exercise. (Indeed, they never did call nor did any one attempt to telephone her after my early intervention when I put Rule 1 in place).

Let us take this letter apart, paragraph by paragraph.

Paragraph 1

'…. agreement your client would have had with (the Bank)'.

It is clear that the Debt Collection Agency has not had sight of any agreement. It is certain *they would have asked for a copy* to strengthen the case they are trying to set out in this letter.

By the way, what is this business about a Credit Card? A Card was issued to Mrs T simply to facilitate *withdrawal* of money from the original loan. No signed agreement? Yet this bank issued a *credit* card? Why is it no one produces the agreement?

You, reader, Mrs T and I are all drawing the same conclusion …..!

Paragraph 3

This agency *admits* that Mrs T has repaid the debt in full.

We agreed that it is highly likely that a signed agreement would include details of 'other charges', interest et al.

We also agree that she would have been liable *if* there was a signed agreement.

Where is it?

Paragraph 4

The Bank has been adding huge charges every month to Mrs T's account. It has created a notional huge sum of money on her account as being legitimately due to them.

If they are so sure she owes them money, why, rather than solve the problem at an early stage, have they let it go on and on?

Simple. Because, as time passes, the alleged sum owed rockets up. If they eventually manage to browbeat Mrs T into submission and she pays them a monthly sum, what a lovely profit for everyone! Except, of course, for Mrs T who would end up in penury – not to mention acute anxiety.

Paragraph 5

So they want *me* to forward proposals, do they?

Inherent in this letter is the notion that Mrs T is my 'client'.

Reader, we know differently. I make no charges whatsoever for assisting Mrs T.

The Debt Collection Agency, the Bank and the rest cannot envisage anyone undertaking to help someone without levying some sort of fee.

Perhaps they think that if Mrs T is paying *me* money, that money should be in *their* coffers.

Since this gang of predators are 'money motivated', they are unable to conceive that I help Mrs T 'free of charge'.

No matter. In the next chapter you will see us move into action after our long silence.

CHAPTER 4

A Satisfactory Result

CHAPTER 4

It is only now that we have sufficient ammunition in terms of facts and motivation that we can compose the 'father and mother' of all letters of complaint.

This we shall send by Recorded Delivery with appropriate photocopies to the Group President of the International Corporation of which our U.K. Commercial Bank is just a subsidiary.

Everything we have done so far has been leading up to this letter to which we must bring all our powers of concentration.

To begin with, I can let you into a secret the recipient of our letter (i.e. the Group President) will never know. It is this: we *really* don't mind if he doesn't reply to our letter; if he does, all well and good.

Our prime targets are here in the U.K.:

a) The Chairman of the Commercial Bank;
b) The Debt Collection Agency.

We want the Chairman to write to us personally and to drop the entire campaign against Mrs T.

We also want to stop the Debt Collection Agency dead in its tracks and for good measure make them worry about losing their own client, the Bank.

Mr ----
President, ---- Banking Corporation
Address -----

AIRMAIL BY RECORDED DELIVERY
LETTER OF COMPLAINT

Dear Sir,

  Mrs T has asked me to write this letter and gives authorisation as follows:

I have appointed Professor Brian Homan to write on my behalf:

| Mrs T | Prof B. Homan | Witness |
| (signature) | (signature) | (signature) |

  This lady has asked me to write to you to explain her situation: she has a dispute with a subsidiary company under your corporate auspice, viz. -----. This subsidiary controls: -----.

  I enclose herewith copies of appropriate relevant correspondence for your perusal. Please note particularly correspondence from a debt collection agency, -----, who it seems have been employed by ----- to retrieve your claimed debt. It should be noted that I am examining this company's status.

  Please note, in addition, Mr President, that the enclosed correspondence which has been posted Recorded Delivery via HM Royal Mail (having naturally retained 'blind' copies for exposure) illustrates that your United Kingdom Chairman has repeatedly and consistently failed even to acknowledge Recorded Delivery letters from Mrs T.

  I have, of course, proof of posting via the Post Office.

  To be noted by yourself, please. Your local (U.K.) Chairman appears to utilise the facility of the U.K. Centre for Phone Calls (Call Centre) to shield calls from the public at large – understandably, of course, from the corporate point of view.

  I have provided sample pertinent background correspondence photocopies for you. All other participants will thus rely on you for any *additional* supportive information.

    Yours sincerely,
    (Prof) B. J. B. Homan

c.c.s UK Chairman (Commercial Bank)
    Debt Collection Agency
    Blind copies as appropriate

Reader's note: Post Office will show you how to complete an *International* recorded signature delivery slip.

ANALYSIS OF THIS LETTER

It is brief. The real weight it carries lies in the extensive copy letters accompanying the *original*.

I highlight the Debt Collection Agency for their part in causing distress to Mrs T but above all I castigate the U.K. Chairman of the Commercial Bank for his part in failing his customer.

Recorded Delivery is highlighted to show that we are very careful to keep copies of the correspondence.

The letter also implies that the recipient may well receive contact from a number of different sources – *unwelcome* contact, he will realise.

We will also acknowledge privately that *WE* HAVE A SOUND GRASP OF THE VALUE OF CALL CENTRES AND HELP LINES IN SHIELDING TOP MANAGEMENT FROM THEIR CUSTOMER'S GRIEVANCES.

When he glances through the supporting correspondence, the Group President will see that we have rumbled the techniques used by the Bank not only to shield itself but also to ensnare members of the public into borrowing money and subjecting themselves to outrageous interest charges because they are already in desperate financial trouble.

Although he is fully aware of all this, he does not want the facts to be exposed to the media and Courts of Justice.

He will *above all* be asking his staff about a signed agreement! Where is this document?

NOTE

I think the 'chief of all the bullies' is going to take a couple of weeks checking the facts with his U.K. Chairman and give him a thorough dressing down for the way his staff and ultimately the Chairman himself have mishandled the affair.

The Group President will then instruct his minions to solve the problem (i.e. keep Mrs T happy). While they attempt to put matters right, he will remain silent. I am increasingly confident that we shall not receive a reply just yet; when we do obtain a response, I think it will not come from the President. We shall see!

PROCEDURE FOR POSTING

You will by now, reader, be aware of the detailed procedure from earlier reference to this subject but it will do no harm to go through it again. It is *essential* that you understand and implement it exactly as shown, until it has become second nature.

a) *Original* of the letter, plus photocopies of correspondence from the U.K. Bank. Photocopied letters from the solicitors and the Debt Collection Agency are to be sent to the President of the International Corporation. Mark the envelope 'for the personal attention of the Group President'. Send it Airmail and International Recorded Delivery Signature. Don't forget to attach the receipt of posting to your master file copy.

b) *Copy* of the *original* of the letter. Put a covering note in, marked solely 'for your information'. Then send this by Recorded Delivery to the U.K. Chairman. Mark the envelope 'Personal attention of the U.K. Chairman: Urgent Information'. Again, attach the receipt to the Chairman's file folder noting and explaining on it 'letter to Group President – this copy to U.K. Chairman, information only'.

c) Copy of the *original* of this letter to the Debt Collection Agency, again with a slip 'for your information only'. Mark the envelope 'Important Information' and send it Recorded Delivery. Keep the receipt/certificate of posting and file it as in b) above.

d) Copy of this letter to solicitors, same procedure as for b) and c) above.

Remember to enter details of cash spent on postage, photocopies, etc, in your cash book, with receipts where possible.

NOTE

Re b), c) and d) above. Since none of these letters enclose copy correspondence (only the U.S. Group President received that) each will be wondering what the copy correspondence consisted of. We will leave them to ponder this question; you may be sure it will perturb them.

Now we sit quietly and wait.

Three weeks go by. Reader, you may permit yourself a smile. We draw ever closer to a conclusion.

As anticipated, there is no response from the Group President. This time, with no further delay, we send the following letter:

RECORDED DELIVERY

Mr ----
President, ---- Banking Corporation
Address -----

Date
My ref to you
(Copy) INTERNATIONAL RECORDED RECEIPT
(signed for on your behalf)
Official receipt retained
Ref: U.K. a/c

SUBJECT: COMPLAINT

Dear Sir,

May I please refer you, sir, to the above-named letter and its enclosed relevant correspondence.

I am disappointed that you have felt unable to reply to my letter. More so, I am upset that you have apparently failed to apprise your U.K. executive of my concern. Not a word from your subordinate senior executive.

Once again, in the final resort, I have had to appeal to my friend Professor Homan to type out for me my absolute annoyance at your appalling lack of good manners, sir.

I have asked the Professor to please illustrate that these are my words. Signatures at the end of this letter show accordingly.

To put the best light on your conduct in this matter, succinctly:

a) Possibly you have not been handed my original letter addressed to you personally?

b) You have indeed read my letter and chosen to pass this to your subordinate, U.K. Chairman / Chief Executive?

c) Such subordinate may have taken a leaf from your book and passed it on to his staff.

d) One or both have chosen to sit back in silence and await an outcome.

Sir, I may be old, crippled and irascible but I retain the integrity of open honesty. Come hell or high water.

Please do not assume that you can make an offer just before we enter Her Majesty's Court of Justice. Should you wish to settle this matter now, I am intrigued as to how you will explain yourself, sir.

I await your response.

    In truth, sincerely
    (signature)
    Mrs T

Signature witnessed
(Address)

Copies as appropriate

ANALYSIS OF THIS LETTER

You will see, of course, that Mrs T has expressed herself in no uncertain terms. That is precisely what is required. The key factor is that the letter illustrates most forcibly her total willingness to take the issue to court.

Briefly, she makes herself quite clear: she is no longer afraid of any of them. The only contribution I had to make was to list for her the points to be raised and put them in order. Her own inimitable style has done the rest.

Within ten days of sending this letter to the Group President, we receive the following reply from the U.K. Managing Director, signed personally:

P O Box -----
Ref: ------
(Date)

Address of recipient

Dear Mrs T,

Re: --------

Thank you for your most recent correspondence.

I am very concerned that you feel that we have not adequately responded to you.

Your letter was passed to us because none of the personnel in the States have access to your account and would not have been able to deal with the issues that you raised. The department that responded to you acts on behalf of the Chief Executive. This is a specialist team who are experienced in handling complaints. I am very sorry if you feel that this has in any way made light of your concerns. This was certainly never our intention.

I would be grateful if you would let me know how you would like to proceed with this matter. I look forward to hearing from you.

Yours sincerely,

(Signature)

ANALYSIS OF THIS LETTER

a) It is addressed personally to Mrs T at her home address.

b) The first paragraph is arrant nonsense and a palpable untruth.

c) The international Group Headquarters, in particular the Board of Directors headed by the global President, can obviously have access to anything and everything relating to any and all of their subsidiaries simply by issuing an instruction. Who does the Managing Director think he is fooling?
This is the very first time we see the word 'sorry'! Not before time.

d) The final paragraph. So they want to know how we would like to proceed?

Do you realise, dear reader, that we have won? Savour the moment!

POST MORTEM

To begin with, readers, I am able to tell you that neither Mrs T nor I have ever heard from this company again.

We did not tell them how we wanted them to proceed simply because they did exactly what we wanted them to do without our having to lift a finger.

Their total silence over the years since that time, plus the fact that they wrote off this alleged debt without attempting to damage Mrs T's future credit rating in any way, speaks volumes.

Never again did we hear from their solicitors or debt collectors.

The Commercial Bank decided wisely not to take Mrs T to court.

I asked Mrs T if she wished to write to them and ask for exemplary damages plus a disclaimer relieving them of the risk of her taking the Bank to court at some date in the future.

Rather than do this, Mrs T felt it would be better from her viewpoint to leave the option of taking them to court open to her. I think she chose sensibly.

Bear in mind that the bank now have a very sharp 'sword of Damocles' hanging over them. If, at some time in the future, they were to choose to re-activate the case and go to court to make a case against Mrs T, they would be foolish in the extreme.

They are aware of this in view of all the climb-downs they have been obliged to make.

These include their inability to provide a copy of any signed document of agreement between themselves and

Mrs T, claiming she owed money when their Debt Collection Agency had acknowledged *in writing* that she had paid the full amount, plus their failure to advise her of the huge interest charges they would apply.

Imagine all this coming out in court! Quite apart from the bad publicity they would receive, a Judge would be likely to penalise them substantially.

Mrs T has also been relieved of terrible stress in connection with the dispute. She now has peace of mind.

Icing on the cake? If Mrs T had not *complained effectively* she may well have given in to the Bank's persistent demands and committed herself to paying for many years to come, money amounting to well in excess of a four-figure sum.

Mrs T is alive, well and happy again!

READER PLEASE NOTE:

This 'case' occurred in 2003 and is a typical example of banks' selling techniques at that time.

Should the appropriate authorities doubt the veracity of this case history, kindly note all of the original correspondence is held by me in safe custody.

(This book is written in 2008) – Author

CHAPTER 5

Faulty Fiasco

CHAPTER 5

We learn. Thank you for accompanying me through a case history which took well over a year before reaching at last, a successful conclusion.

That particular case, dear reader, was about as tough as it gets.

Now, to raise your spirits and renew your enthusiasm, you are about to see in the course of this chapter how efficient we are becoming at *complaining effectively*.

As always: settle your thoughts. Gradually, with discipline, planning and attention to detail, your thought processes are inexorably adjusting to the habit of making logical progressions. This bodes well for the future.

The complaint we are about to examine presents a number of features quite different from those of the previous problem.

May I please remind you that courtesy and firmness are essential from day one. This time we shall examine how a major U.K. based international company that is well run and customer orientated can deal with a complaint. Such an organisation puts customer satisfaction as its first priority.

Nevertheless, we must always adhere to our own procedure because it is by following *our own rules* that the ethics of the company become apparent. We learn about the company in question by analysing its responses and the principles underlying them, thus perhaps intuiting more than may be realised …

THE BACKGROUND SCENARIO

A friend telephoned in some distress, telling me that his wife was in tears. She had, it seems, been saving up for some time to visit London in order to buy a number of different items from a well-known clothing store. These items comprised a mixture of treats for herself and gifts for her friends.

For this married lady who lived a quiet life in the country the trip to London was a major event, particularly because she was to make the journey alone. The latter proved uneventful. Arriving at the store, she proceeded to make her purchases.

At this point it is relevant to note that each item of clothing was on display and a *sample* could be examined before the purchase was made of a (presumably) identical but *pre-packed* item in the appropriate size and colour.

Having made her choice, the lady paid cash and received an itemised sales receipt which she retained.

On returning home after a round trip of almost three hundred miles, she unwrapped each item, setting to one side for gift wrapping, the purchases intended for her friends.

Imagine her distress on discovering, after careful examination of each individual item, that three of them had serious manufacturing faults!

Her husband had telephoned me as a good friend, aware that I was researching examples of complaints for analysis. Neither he nor his wife had so far given any thought as to how they proposed to complain.

Offering to help, I spoke to my friend's wife (whom I shall call Molly) and agreed with her that I should complain on her behalf. It was arranged that I should call to see her that evening having explained that I would prefer to deal solely with her in this matter: a three-way conversation debating the subject would only confuse the issue.

Remember, reader: only deal with the complainant! If you bring anyone else into the complaint process you are asking for trouble.

That evening, Molly's husband having agreed my point, I went through the initial procedure.

We are familiar with the process by now.

As this complaint was to be initiated by me from the word go, no (already) existing problems of telephone calls or correspondence presented themselves.

The lady would make no telephone calls to the company, nor would she accept any from them (see our previously outlined Rules).

Having agreed these conditions Molly said she would explain the reasons for them to her husband. He telephoned the next day to assure me that he would abide by his wife's wishes and was perfectly content to do so.

Molly gave me her *written authorisation*, witnessed by her husband, to act on her behalf.

Reader, you will understand the importance of clarifying at the outset, simply and clearly, *why* it is so important to deal only with the complainant. It would only take a protective husband (or wife, or anyone else) to contribute their 'two pennyworth' consisting perhaps of an angry telephone call or an emotive or aggressive letter, for the whole of our Effective Complaint process to collapse in disarray.

Please remember, if you discuss your problem with anyone else, it is *your* complaint that will go awry if you lose control of the situation. You are complaining *on your own behalf*. Permit no outside influence to intrude.

RULE 6

KEEP THE COMPLAINT TO YOURSELF

Do not discuss it with *anyone at all.*

Molly gave me the following essential details:

a) Total travel costs incurred in her round trip to London.

b) Meal costs

c) Estimated postage and packaging costs should it be necessary to return some or all of the items purchased to the store in London, to a branch store, or to the different manufacturers who supplied the items to the store. I could not, of course, check on the possible costs should it become necessary to send each item back to a supplying manufacturer but that would be something to bear in mind should we need to do this. At the same time, if this *did* occur, a claim for such costs would be made against the supplying store.

Another point for consideration here is that if we should run into difficulties with a claim against the store, the individual suppliers – the manufacturers – would be a useful second string in such an eventuality.

d) I noted that, of the seven individual items purchased, three were found to have manufacturing defects. The value of these items was totalled separately from that of the perfect ones.

e) A key factor was that Molly had retained the till receipt marked 'paid in cash' and listing the goods individually.

In complaints of this nature, it is worth considering whether to complain directly to each individual manufacturer at the very beginning with a copy of each separate complaint (posted, of course, Recorded Delivery) being sent to the store's Group Chairman, accompanied by a supporting covering letter *or* to begin with a complaint direct to the Chairman.

From personal experience – and I have tried both of the above methods – I have found it wiser to take the route of a direct letter to the store's Group Chairman.

Having established in the manner explained earlier the name and full Head Office address of the Chairman, we compose the following letter:

RECORDED DELIVERY

My name, (per pro 'Molly')
My address
(Date)

Group Chairman's, name
Company's Head Office address

COMPLAINT

Dear ----

     As you will see from the attached (copy) authorisation I have been asked to write to you personally concerning a complaint by Mrs ----- .
     She purchased the following items for cash from your London main store on (date): see enclosed photocopy of the sales receipt herewith which lists the individual items.
     Those items which she has marked * on the receipt are of faulty manufacture. The unmarked items were satisfactory.
     Mrs ----- felt it unnecessary at the time of purchase to open each packaged item because she was able to examine a sample of each one *unpackaged* shown for sales purposes, on display. These were all in perfect condition, so she felt it was only necessary to choose size and colour from the ready-packaged range. Naturally, I have not arranged to dispatch the faulty items to you at this stage; I will wait until I hear from you.
     Mrs ----- is extremely surprised that your quality control department has allowed standards to slip and I should mention that she was reduced to tears over the whole sorry episode.
     You will, I am sure, sympathise with her as her visit to your store was her first unaccompanied trip. She feels extremely vulnerable at the prospect of another expensive journey to London to return the goods personally.
     She points out that your nearest branch store to her home is relatively small and has a limited range of goods in comparison with your London flag-ship store and that, even if you wanted her

to return the goods in person to this local store she would have to travel by bus and train (a round trip of ninety miles) to return the items.

Finally she mentions that two of the items were intended as birthday gifts thus compounding her distress!

I list below the costs Mrs ----- has incurred to date in this matter:

--- / London return journey   £ -
Taxi fare from London terminus   £ -
(to and from your store)
* Three faulty items   £ - (total of three)
Estimated cost of return of goods   £ -
By parcel post (recorded)

She has not as yet included travel costs should she be required to return the goods *personally*.

Thank you, sir, in anticipation of your sympathetic and immediate attention to this matter.

Yours sincerely,

Per pro 'Molly'
Brian Homan

Enc.   1.   Sales receipt (photocopy)
         2.   Letter of authorisation to act on behalf of Mrs ---

ANALYSIS OF THIS LETTER

a) It is important to establish from the outset that Molly holds the *original* sales receipt. Without that, it would be much more difficult (though not impossible) to validate a claim against the store.

b) Molly shows that she is being honest and open by illustrating that though three items were of faulty manufacture the balance of the purchase was fine.

c) We are not blaming the store's staff. How could they know that a sealed package would contain a faulty item?

d) We have *intimated* that we require *a refund of cash* for the faulty items. We do not want them exchanged.

e) We have made especially clear that we think Molly should not have had to open on the spot each individually packaged item, sealed as it was. After all, there was a sample which had been made available for inspection by the customer and checked for possible faults.

f) By holding on to the faulty goods awaiting the Chairman's response, Molly retains the *evidence* of her claim. She awaits 'instructions' (i.e. an offer of compensation) from the Chairman before doing anything.

g) Note that I have illustrated the availability of evidence, in the unlikely event that the Chairman would expect her to return the goods in person. This does, however, serve as an example of the stressful possibilities envisaged by M. *She did*, in fact, think that she might be obliged to return the goods in person to get her money back.

I will now go over with you, once again, the postal procedure to be employed to ensure that it is becoming an *automatic* response. There must be no deviation from our Rules and methods.

The original letter is sent to the named Chairman of the company at the Head Office. Do check carefully that it *is* the Head Office: you will recall that if these details are not shown at their web site (see Library/Computers) and if the *Registered Office* is not shown, apply by letter to Companies House who will at least provide you with the details of the Registered Office to apply to.

The letter and envelope are both marked Recorded Delivery and additionally, on the envelope, you write: 'For the Personal Attention of Mr ---, Chairman', with of course the full address. Take this to the Post Office and retain their official receipt and certificate of posting.

Enter all costs into your cash book.

Mark dispatch date / Company name on your calendar and do not forget to mark up dates of incoming letters from the company as and when such letters arrive.

Open a fresh file for your complaint, keep a copy of the letter and postal receipt in the file.

(Note: I hope you do not have to Complain Effectively too often …!)

At this point it is timely to remind you that in all letters you write in the course of a complaint, you observe Rule 7:

RULE 7

Never provide your opponent(s) with ammunition in the form of any information concerning your *future actions* in the course of lodging a given complaint.

Within a few days of sending our letter, I received a reply from the head of Corporate Affairs at their central London Head Office.

Before taking any action on the matter I verified that this person reports directly – in person – to the Stores Group Chairman.

I obtained this information by our standard method (see previous pages), i.e. by making an anonymous call to the switchboard at the Head Office asking simply 'What position does Mr --- hold in your company, please? I wish to write to him.' (I was given full details as well as those of the Chairman himself).

Please remember that this is one of the very few situations in which you are permitted to deviate from one of our Rules – No telephone contact!

Now, dear reader, study the following letter. It seems we are dealing with a thoroughly reputable company which is taking immediate action to deal with M's complaint.

Company's name
Address
(Date)
Ref no ---

Dear Mr -----

Thank you for contacting me. I was sorry to hear of Mrs -----disappointment with recent purchases from ----- (name of store).

To enable me to investigate this matter fully, I would be grateful if you would return the merchandise to me at the above address at your earliest convenience. I can assure you that I will reimburse any postal and travel expenses you have incurred as a result of your complaint, when I write to you again.

Thank you for helping in this way and I hope to hear from you soon.

Yours sincerely

(signature)

Corporate Affairs

Interestingly, this gentleman sent his letter to Molly's home address whilst marking it c/o myself. He is making sure that both she and I are jointly kept fully informed. A thoughtful and sensible touch.

Next I arranged with Molly to send the faulty merchandise to the company's Head Office for inspection as requested.

It is unusual to see that the Head Office of this company is also their Registered Office as their company's letter heading shows; this is most open and reassuring. Obviously, I am unable to show you the actual letter-heading for reasons of confidentiality.

It is heartening to see that the company is offering to reimburse Molly's postal and travel expenses.

At this point, an unfortunate 'hiccup' occurs. Although our system is working well, Molly, still upset, now decides to make a day return trip to obtain a full refund from the group's local store, taking with her *all* the items purchased from their main London Store.

She explained to me that *she* thought it the best thing to do … Say no more!

My reaction was that at least she had received all her purchase money back and felt a little better: that was what mattered to her.

Imagine, then, my astonishment when a further letter arrived from our gentleman at Head Office. This one says it all!

Company's name and address
Telephone no.
Date
Ref no ---

Address of Mrs ---

Dear Sir,

I was sorry to learn of your disappointment with several items purchased from our store. Please accept my sincere apologies for the obvious concern and inconvenience this matter has caused.

I would like to assure you that we constantly strain to maintain and improve the standards of quality which our customers have come to expect. We work very closely with our suppliers and insist on stringent quality control measures, which apply throughout manufacture, to ensure our merchandise meets our requirements. I very much regret that despite this care, you have experienced problems of this nature. Having found so many faults, I accept that you feel our quality has dropped. Nevertheless, I assure you that it remains our priority to maintain and improve our quality control and as such I have passed details of your complaint to colleagues in the Buying Department concerned.

In the meantime, Mrs ---, I enclose a cheque to the value of £-- as a refund for the faulty items you have *not been able to return to the store* and to reimburse the expenses you have incurred as a result of this matter. As I am sure you will appreciate, it will help our quality control team a great deal to have the opportunity to examine the faulty garments. Could I therefore ask you to return the garments to me at the above address. I have included an additional amount to pay for the garments to be sent to me.

Once again, thank you for taking the time and trouble to bring this matter to my attention. I do hope that, despite your recent disappointment, you will remain a valued customer.

Yours sincerely
(signature)

Corporate affairs

c.c.   B J Homan

Our gentleman at Head Office is obviously unaware that in the interim Molly has taken the matter out of his and my hands by gaining a *full* cash refund from one of the firm's provincial stores!

To cap it all, hot on the heels of this last letter, a third arrives.

Company's name and address
Telephone no.
Date
Ref no ---

Dear Mrs ---

    I am in receipt of Prof. Homan's letter of the (date) relating to our previous correspondence regarding your disappointment with merchandise recently purchased from our stores.
    I now understand that you were able to return the faulty items to our --- store and that you have been fully reimbursed. In view of this, as I do not wish to cause you any further inconvenience, there is no need to return the cheque for £ -- that I sent as a refund for these garments. I do hope you will keep this with my compliments and as a sincere gesture of goodwill. However, it would appear that you have not been refunded for the cost of the slip which has now been returned and as such I enclose vouchers to the value of £ --.
    Once again, Mrs ---, I would like to thank you for taking the trouble to contact us. I do hope that this matter has now been concluded to your satisfaction.

    Yours sincerely
    (signature)

    Corporate Affairs

More confusion! I understood Molly had returned *all* the items to the provincial store since she had definitely received a total refund for all the items purchased. Now we learn that she failed to return one faulty item but that she eventually did post this on to them..

Nevertheless, Head Office asked her to retain the original substantial cheque they sent her with their compliments in addition to the cash refund she received.

Finally, as icing on the cake, they sent her £15.00 in vouchers to spend on their goods in store.

The final outcome of this remarkable sequence of events was that Molly received hundreds of pounds in compensation.

No negotiation was required. This company, acting of its own volition had resolved this customer complaint in an exemplary manner, whilst thanking us for drawing attention to Molly's problem. It showed willingness to examine possible faults in their business and full understanding of their customer's point of view.

What a difference from the attitude of those senior executives in international conglomerates who seem hell bent on shielding themselves and their board of directors from dealing directly with customers. In companies such as these, the ethos appears to be to expand the business at any cost, satisfy the shareholders whilst keeping existing customers quiet and 'in the bag'. We

may with justification ascribe to these companies a motto of 'Us first *and then* them'.
Consider other aspects of these greedy companies.

If their products and services offered to the public were well researched and produced to a high standard of quality before being released for sale – always allowing for an occasional 'blip' in the system – there would be little need for 'help lines' that exist merely to obfuscate and delay – and possibly exhaust into silence – both new and existing customers.

The mushrooming of Call Centres is a prime example of companies attempting to ring-fence themselves against problems with customers.

Companies who use Call Centres offer several flawed reasons for setting them up. You will hear them protest that if only the customer would read the small print in their agreements, problems would not occur. However, a sales person exerting high pressure in the presence of a customer who has been persuaded he needs a new conservatory is scarcely likely to go through the small print with that customer. Sales agents are in the business of *selling* not providing a caring and thoughtful service to the potential buyer.

Another reason (for which read 'excuse') for the setting up of a Call Centre is that because of the demand for the products/services, occasional complaints are bound to arise – *occasionally*, of course – due to the sheer volume of customers involved. The implication is that problems increase exponentially as customer volume expands. Sounds, logical, doesn't it? In that case, how was it that in our last case history concerning a global organisation the complaint was dealt with at National Head Office level?

I would like to think that this was because we know how to *Complain Effectively*. To some extent this is true, in the case of excellent companies such as the one we last dealt with, but it so happens that that particular international group *does not have a Call Centre.*

They have a small department 'in house' of dedicated staff available to help any customer with a complaint. Yes we received four star treatment from the executive in charge of the specially highly trained staff because we directed our complaint to the Chairman. However, it is my belief that *in this case* our complaint would have been dealt with perfectly efficiently had a lower level of management been involved.

Never forget, dear reader, Call Centres / help lines exist because of ever increasing numbers of customers complaints.

CHAPTER 6

Ticket to Ride

CHAPTER 6

So far, we have dealt successfully with two complaints and illustrated both the difficulties experienced with the first and the helpful simplicities of the second.

We will now examine a complaint which *could* have been resolved quickly.

It illustrates the problem of a person who has paid in full, in advance, for a promised service from a well-known, high-profile national company which specifies in its advertising campaigns, the trouble-free processing of customers' orders, takes the money, then fails to deliver on a promise.

The point here is to illustrate how to *win* when the complainant has *already used the company Help Line*: we are going to have to pick up the pieces when the complaint goes wrong.

The value of this example is that you yourself may already be in the position of being half-way through making a complaint and finding it is not proceeding in accordance with your expectations.

THE STORY OF MISS L

Incidentally, before I begin, may I point out that not all the complaints I have dealt with emanate from the fair sex, merely a substantial majority! The reasons why this should be so do not fall within my remit: perhaps my readers will have views on the matter?

Now for Miss L, who intended to travel from A to B by rail on a specific day and month. This requirement is specified in *her* letter of complaint to the company, as you will see:

RECORDED DELIVERY

Name
Address
Date

Without Prejudice

The Help Line
Refunds Department

Sir/Madam,

    This letter and enclosure are photocopied and will be sent if necessary to the --- Trains, C.E.O. (Chief Executive Officer) and the B.B.C. – *if necessary*.
    I ordered against Direct Debit a one-way ticket from Oxford to Paignton *expressly stating* the ticket must be available for use *on any day during the next month*.
    Availability was to commence (date).
    After over 30 minutes on the 'phone I was assured by your agent that although my request was unusual, they, after much internal discussion, agreed that it was OK.
    So I gave authorisation to charge against my card. I am appalled to see that what has been issued is a single ticket for use *only* on (date).
    Not only do I insist on an immediate refund and waiver of your £-- standard administration charge, but in addition I shall require *subsequently* an ex-gratia payment of £140.
    Just because I'm very angry I have still my wits about. (sic)

    Yours in anger

    (Miss L)

Encls. Copy of Post Office Recorded Delivery receipt.

ANALYSIS OF THIS LETTER

a) It will be clear to the reader that I was asked by Miss L to help her *after* she had launched this tirade. The above is an *exact* copy of Miss L's letter!

b) She is a very feisty lady and had 'done her own thing', as the saying goes – indeed she had got the Recorded Delivery bit right for a start!

c) She is *very* angry and certainly puts her feelings about the matter strongly in writing.

d) She appears to have some idea of How to Complain – but not Effectively.

e) Above all, Miss L has put the cart before the horse by threatening to report the matter to the C.E.O. or Managing Director should the Helpline fail to accede to her demands.

f) You will see that she marks the letter 'without prejudice'. Putting this at the top of a letter usually means that the writer is considering the possibility of taking the matter to a Court of Justice and that the letter cannot be produced as evidence. This tells me she is prepared to do just that if she does not get her way at this stage.

g) Her ex-gratia payment claim is way over the top.

What has she done wrong?

Apart from sending her letter to their Help Line she has made the mistake of writing in an emotional, angry, threatening tone to a clerk who will not feel like being very helpful after receiving it.

We would certainly not make these mistakes, would we, dear reader, after reading the preceding pages? I hope not!

The good news, however, is that Miss L provided me with a photocopy of her original letter as well as a copy of the Post Office receipt for sending the original by Recorded Delivery.

My first step was to send another copy of this letter to the *same* address, this time accompanied by my authorisation to act on her behalf. Nothing else was mentioned in my covering letter which accompanied the authorisation. The important aim at this stage was to put Miss L back into our standard procedure.

My second action was to send another copy of Miss L's letter to the Chairman of the company with a brief covering note illustrating my authorisation to act on her behalf and adding simply 'for your information'.

You will see that we are attempting to retrieve the situation by not volunteering any further information: Miss L has provided the facts already. Now we await a

response, ideally from the Chairman. We shall certainly receive one from their Refunds department.
Sure enough it arrives.

Company Name

Travel Centre

Professor B.J.B. Homan
Address

Date
Our Ref: ---

Dear Professor Homan

Thank you for the application for a refund.

The cost of the ticket purchased was £--. A standard clerical fee has been deducted therefore a refund of £-- is payable.

I have sent details to our Head Office at ----- where a cheque for £-- will be produced for you. If you do not receive the cheque within 15 working days please phone ------.

Yours sincerely,
(signature)

Refunds

ANALYSIS OF THIS LETTER

a) It could be that Miss L's letter has upset the Refund department's staff. This letter is addressed to me with no reference to her.

b) They reiterate their right to charge a standard fee despite the certainty that they are responsible for the original error.

c) Nevertheless they claim to be sending a cheque for the cost of the ticket minus a standard administration charge.

I maintain absolute silence in response to this letter. Two weeks elapse and despite their request for us to telephone them if the promised cheque fails to arrive, silence is maintained.

The cheque finally arrives a week later, made out to *me*. They certainly want nothing to do with Miss L!

She agrees with my suggestion that we do not cash the cheque and maintain our silence.

The strategy here is to play a waiting game, simply to see if the Chairman is going to come up with something. Perhaps he has not taken notice of Miss L's declared intentions concerning Court proceedings and media exposure.

It took a further three weeks of silence before Miss L (not I) received a pleasant surprise.
A First Class Open return ticket for Miss L's original journey, accompanied by a compliments slip from the Chairman's office!

So he *had* taken action on her letter, whilst allowing his Help Line to do its own thing.

You will recall that Miss L's original ticket was for a *single* journey.

In addition, since it was an O*pen* ticket Miss L – you guessed it – claimed a refund on it.

This she received promptly.

I returned their original cheque, payable to me, direct to the Chairman's office with a simple covering note expressing Miss L's warmest thanks.

Sometimes, dear reader, one just has to smile.

What a sensible Chairman!

CHAPTER 7

Staying on Track

CHAPTER 7

In the preceding chapters we have seen that *money* has been the predominant factor of recompense in COMPLAINING EFFECTIVELY.

You will now begin to realise how proficient you are becoming in using our rules and detailed procedures to ensure that you *win*.

My selected targets have embodied both 'goodies' and 'baddies' in terms of the companies incurring our displeasure. You are aware by now of the importance of maintaining – at all times – strict discipline and an unemotional approach to the problems confronting you.

As you are aware, action has been taken *on behalf of the complainant* in all the case histories described so far. *Your* need, dear reader, is to secure a satisfactory solution to *your own problem* and to use this book as a point of referral should you require to complain effectively at any time in the future.

Had this book been based on my own few personal experiences, it would have been severely limited in scope and at the same time open to a charge of self-aggrandisement.

My aim is simple; to provide a diversity of examples collated and studied over a period of many years exposing categories of areas of dispute as well as *factual* material showing specifically *how* and *why* our procedures really work.

You will have realised how much easier it is to *complain effectively* in the very early stages of your predicament: it is more than likely that you have picked up this book at the stage where you are contemplating the initiation of a complaint, but it could be that you need help in getting to grips with a situation already in existence. You may have made already, some of the classic mistakes, but *you* are now equipped with the know-how to set about rectifying the situation and proceed with confidence.

It is, of course, difficult to change your method of approach and review the situation calmly in the light of an objective reassessment of the situation, but you can be sure that success *is* achievable even when you have reached the stage where things do not appear to be going in your favour.

Whatever your position, whether starting from scratch or already involved in a seemingly losing battle, you may be confident that when you reach the last page of this book you will be in control and *win*!

YOUR OWN PROBLEM

It is worthwhile to examine in greater depth, your own feelings of grievance and anger, even at the risk of going over ground already covered in the preceding chapters of this book. Indeed, if you are already mid-way into your complaint process, switching to the Effective Complaint method may at first seem well-nigh impossible. Take heart – the seamless fusion of two different approaches can be achieved by the following means:

a) Stop any further contact with your opponent(s) *immediately*, except by Recorded Delivery letter.

b) Implement at once our telephone policy according to the Rule: no response to incoming calls from the opposition.

c) From now on, talk to *no one* about your problem. Quite apart from boring them to death, you will receive inevitably advice, good bad or indifferent; its effect will be to clutter and confuse your mind. Already in turmoil.

a), b) and c) are designed to give *yourself* a break. I am not suggesting that you take a few days off, but that you use this time to sort out all existing correspondence and write down from memory all phone conversations. Then put everything into date order with earliest dates on top.

If you decide (and why not?) to go away for a few days on your own, take all the relevant papers with you. The 'break' is not intended to be a holiday!

Whatever you do, *do not open any incoming mail*. If it has a bearing on your complaint you will have enough to worry about already without adding to your anxiety. Do not forget to ignore any e-mails from your opponent; put them aside *unread*.

Have you listed all related expenses to date in your cash book? If not, do it now. Shut yourself in a room where you will not be disturbed. Lock the door if necessary. Make it crystal clear that there must be no interruptions from well-meaning family or friends! Much as you love them all, you must keep yourself to yourself whilst you begin the process of calming down and clearing your mind. Not easy if you are unaccustomed to it, but essential none the less.

Now. In splendid isolation, you can examine carefully every piece of information that has passed between you and your antagonist.

In every case, analyse the communication and jot down your assessment on a separate piece of paper.

You are looking out for the following elements, both in the opponent's and *your own* communications: emotional words/phrases, allegations, accusations, assumptions, downright errors, implications, double meanings, evasions, denials, lies, threats (overt or covert), inconsistencies, promises or guarantees.

When you have noted down on your separate sheet or sheets of paper any of these pertaining to each individual communication, a picture will begin to emerge. This will reveal to you what you're up against as well as what *you yourself* have said or committed to paper. How does the image of your opponent compare to your own?

a) Are *you* absolutely right or partially in the right?

b) Is your opponent absolutely right or partially in the right?

You are responsible for assessing a) and b) separately, fairly and *honestly*.

Before you judge yourself too harshly however, just consider the following: Have you been misled in any way? Have 'they' treated you without consideration? Did they actually deceive you? Did you perhaps not understand what was going on?

Having analysed the situation, you are able to put down in writing the *exact* nature of your complaint. You may say that you have done this already and that I am underestimating your intelligence! Not in the least – all I ask is that you reflect *in depth* on the nature of your complaint. You can then be one hundred per cent certain about the type of complaint you are making. Should you not have made this obvious in your previous correspondence (especially if it is in any respect different from the complaint you have been making) this is your chance to get back on track.

A simple way of putting things right is to prepare a Recorded Delivery letter on the following lines:

Dear -----

     I refer to previous correspondence in the matter of (refer to the earlier letters/phone calls which have gone before).
     For clarification purposes, please note the following: (here write down concisely what it is you are complaining about).
     Yours faithfully etc.

In sending this letter, you have negated all earlier discussions connected with your complaint. This is how it works: should 'they' write to you in the future and refer to any earlier letters or telephone calls from you, simply write back referring to the letter you have just written. You need not respond to anything arising from past exchanges between you, but *you yourself* maintain the right to refer to anything either you or they have declared previously.

In this way you achieve two important objectives:

a)   You have initiated a fresh start for yourself.

b)   You will 'peeve' the opposition by gaining the initiative as regards responding to their tactics by using past communications to back up your arguments. Should they attempt to do the same thing, they will be met with silence until *you* decide to reply. You may choose to respond with a fresh point in your favour or on the other hand, you may continue to remain silent for the time being. This achievement should afford you the satisfaction of knowing that during your 'break' you have taken control of the situation and seamlessly bonded your earlier approach to our disciplined behaviour. More power to your elbow!

CHAPTER 8

Trade Secrets

CHAPTER 8

SERVICES

Under this heading I include individuals as well as companies who provide a service. In this area of activity, you the customer are being sold an *idea*, namely the idea that the service company (or individual) will do a job of work for you in exchange for payment. You may think that nothing could be more obvious, but remember that you should only be expected to pay for the service when the work has been COMPLETED. If you buy an apple, you pay for it when it is in your hand, after inspecting it. Only then do you hand over payment.

Why is it, then, that people are so gullible that they will often part with all or a proportion of the quoted cost either before the work has even been started or make part payments as it proceeds? Think of builders, double glazing salesmen, plumbers, etc. They will all claim, inevitably, to do a good job of work at a competitive price, but then they would, wouldn't they?

We know differently. Of course, there are large numbers of excellent service providers, both 'one-man bands' and large well-established companies who do good work at a reasonable price. We also know that there exist a number of confidence tricksters – not just the 'one-man band' but whole companies dedicated to relieving you of your money for a job never started, partially completed, or so-called 'finished work' of poor quality.

How do we separate the wheat from the chaff?

QUOTATIONS

Before selecting a person or company to do a job for you, ask friends and neighbours if they can recommend someone – not just someone they've *heard* does a good job. If you have to extend your enquiries, perhaps through the telephone directory, check for companies in your own locality.

Always check if there is a call-out charge! You may be surprised to learn that there are individuals who make a fat living out of call-out charges alone. They insist on cash, make a show of examining the problem, quote a most reasonable price , take your cash – and flee! They are never seen again; having promised to start the next day and given a spurious business card to inspire confidence in their good faith. The telephone number you were given will never be a well-established one and their address will be bogus, I will not enlarge upon how they set up this scam – suffice it to say that they achieve their aim of obtaining cash from you, if not on the day of their visit; they will return when you have got the money together! They may even appear to start work, but rest assured they will be off the minute they have obtained that call-out charge.

Other tricksters will not ask for the call-out charge at once. They will actually start work, or even complete it but the final bill will be extortionate. When you complain, they often become threatening, then reduce the bill a little and suggest they will un-do the work unless you pay up.

Let us, dear reader, start right at the beginning, to *prevent* such scams.

a) Avoid *all* service providers who insist on a call-out charge. Out there you will find a number who do not require such a fee.

b) Whoever you ask into your home for a quote, be they highly recommended or not, be absolutely sure NEVER to leave them alone in your property. Watch them unobtrusively, constantly. Temptation is always there, even if most do not succumb to it. You may relax a little if and when you decide to use their services and get to know them better, but stay on your guard.

c) Have a trusted friend with you when a prospective workman visits for the first time to give you a price for the job.

   Having received the quote, under no circumstances agree to having the job done on a first visit. Tell the person you will decide in a day or two.

d) Obtain *at least* two quotes for the job.

e) When you think you have the right person, *begin your checks on them*. It is wise to make checks on all those quoting.

f) Your checks should be: samples of their work to be seen locally. If they have not worked locally, ask for the names, addresses and telephone numbers of a couple of people they have done work for. Even if you cannot physically check on the quality of their work, at least you can get an opinion.

If your reasonable request is denied or agreed to grudgingly think long and hard before you agree to employ them. I for one would have grave doubts. After all, why should they not be proud of their achievements?

g) To be really thorough in your checking, contact one of the national credit-worthiness agencies. You can obtain a swift answer for pennies. I recommend it.

h) Gain agreement from your chosen service provider that you will pay in full only upon *satisfactory completion* of the work. Emphasise that it must be to *your* satisfaction, not theirs. Also ensure that under no circumstances will you be prepared to make any partial payments whilst the work to be done is incomplete. Write down these conditions on a sheet of paper and ask them to sign, address and date this together with your own details and signature. Ask your friend to do the same as witness to the agreement.

This may sound like a great deal of work just to get a simple job done. *It is not a great deal of work.* A few minutes' effort will save you a great deal of trouble in terms of time, worry and stress if things should go wrong.

When everything is completed and to your satisfaction, don't forget to provide your name and address to the service provider as a reference. You will have made a friend for life.

EMERGENCY REPAIRS

… and I mean *real* emergencies! Common sense will tell you that in dire emergency you contact Police, Fire, Ambulance at once. Follow your 999 call by contacting the appropriate Public Utility service provider – gas, water, electricity. After which, in the case of damage caused to home or contents, naturally you contact your insurance company. Make sure you have cover – so many people think it is just another unnecessary expense, until of course, you *need* the cover!

PROBLEMS

If, despite my warning (or if they have come too late for you) you have parted with money to a service provider and feel duped for whatever reason, appropriate action must be taken.

Let us suppose, for example, that you have paid an instalment part-way through the job to be done, or that the work has been completed to a very poor standard – discovered only after you have paid for it in full. In the latter case, it can be useful to buy a cheap disposable camera if your mobile telephone does not double up as a photographic device.

Where possible, photographs should be taken before and after completion of the work. They can provide a very useful adjunct in helping to validate your complaint.

Remember to note on the back of any print the date, time, location and nature of the work done. Remember to take your photographs when no one else is present! Such photographs will lend added support to your Recorded Delivery letter. Discipline and procedure again, dear reader, not forgetting our Rules. I smile with gentle amusement as I hear you sigh … but your aim is to complain EFFECTIVELY, is it not?

Reiterating my assumption that you were not aware of my fore-going list of precautionary measures, or that despite them you handed over money, it is reasonable to assume that you did at least obtain some sort of receipt for the money and that the receipt showed the name, address and telephone number of your unsatisfactory tradesman (or trades-*person* if you must). If you failed to do so, surely you have retained the telephone number by means of which you first contacted him?

(If our chap has just disappeared with your cash and you have *nothing* to help you locate him, you will at least, I trust, have learned an expensive lesson. But of course you DO have those all-important details…?)

This is your course of action:

Do not waste your time telephoning him, even when you know he is almost certainly there.

Send a Recorded Delivery letter to the address shown. Remember, if it is signed for, someone has put a signature to it!

This is your sample letter:

RECORDED DELIVERY

                              Your name and Address Date

His/Her name or trading name
Address

Dear ---

You agreed with me to do work at (give location) commencing on (date) to be completed by (date) for an agreed price of (amount) subject to the work being completed to my satisfaction in every respect.

(List precise details of the work agreed to be done).

Having paid you £--- for the work (* partially) completed in (* part) full (* delete as applicable), I am complaining in that such work as has been done is unsatisfactory and illustrate by this letter my total dissatisfaction at the lack of care/workmanship/damage to my home/rubbish left/delay in this matter and especially your failure to complete the work to an acceptable standard. (You may vary the above to fit your own case).

You have 14 days from the date of this letter to return the money I have paid. Should you do so, no further action will be taken.

No excuses or promises of completion in due course will be acceptable.

Yours faithfully

You now allow the fourteen days to elapse. Do not for one moment expect any response to the above letter! Do, however, set in motion immediate contact with Royal Mail to validate whether they have a signature for your letter. Point out the need for a quick response. This can result in a separate avenue for you to pursue (via the Police) if necessary.

After the fourteen days have elapsed with no response, send, on day fifteen, the second letter.

RECORDED DELIVERY
(WITHOUT PREJUDICE)

Your name and address
Date

His/Her name or trading name
Address

Sir,

      I refer to my letter sent Recorded Delivery to your address on (date).

      You have failed to respond by letter or indeed any form of communication.

      I shall not waste further time on this matter. This letter constitutes formal notification to you that within seven days from today the following steps will be taken:

      A leaflet illustrating your behaviour is being directed to local traders, neighbours and other outlets (including the press) illustrating the situation and naming you personally.

      Note especially that the Police are to be informed.

      The above steps will be implemented on (give date of the seventh day following).

      Should I receive cash to the full amount I have paid you within the next *seven days* plus a written apology, I am prepared to consider the matter closed.

      I repeat you have seven days only.

      Yours faithfully

ANALYSIS OF THIS SECOND LETTER

a) Note the letter is headed both Recorded Delivery *and* Without Prejudice. The letter ensures that you are in the clear to proceed with an action in the Small Claims Court and that the letter is overlooked by the Court when considering your claim.

b) You also have the option of involving the Police.

c) The leaflet costs very little. Draft details of the leaflet yourself, simply stating what has happened. Any 'office shop' will set it up and do the layout for literally just a few pounds – you can then photocopy as few or as many as you wish to do the job.

d) We have pointed out the advantage to him of paying up, as well as the very real disadvantage to him in terms of reputation, business loss and Police action.

e) It is important that the tone of this letter is kept both calm and decisive.

f) We have left him no room for discussion or negotiation.

g) Be certain to carry through your promise to deliver the leaflet as stated in the letter.

THE LEAFLET

Mr X (name in upper case)
Trading as: -------- U/Case (Name)
Address: ------- U/Case

The above named person quoted a price of £--- to effect repairs comprising (state the work quoted for).

Having partly completed the work, he demanded a substantial proportion of the money quoted for the entire job, in CASH.

In good faith and trust I paid him, fearing that if I did not do so he would not complete the work.

He has taken the money but failed to carry out the work to completion.

Please warn your friends and acquaintances that it is unsafe to have dealings with (NAME *AND TRADE NAME* if this is different).

Print and sign your name.

If you wish, give your address or contact number.

Sign and date the leaflet.

Naturally you will keep copies of your letter and the leaflet in your file, with the receipt for your payment (you *have*, of course, carefully preserved this document).

In addition, keep on file details of the leaflet *distribution list*.

As usual, list all expenses incurred in your cash book.

If you have reached the stage where you have been obliged to do all of the above, dear reader, it is abundantly clear that your rogue trader has not paid up.

The next stage is up to you.

Should you decide to set the matter before the Small Claims Court, you will be claiming not only the cash you have paid out but also the additional expenses you have incurred in attempting to get your money back. Don't forget you had felt under threat, because, had you not paid up, the job would never have been completed. You hoped the cash payment would ensure continuance of the work to be done, did you not?

If the case is stated, I would not hesitate to bring the claim before the Small Claims Court. Should you decide to do so, obtain the form of application to the Court (phone clerk to local Court for this) – it is a straightforward business.

However, although you go on to win the case, this does not always mean that your opponent will automatically pay up. Such petty villains often use a number of ruses to evade payment and even when they have a court judgement against them, legally binding them to pay up, they may promise to pay in instalments, frequently failing to do so. They may plead that they can only afford to pay a paltry sum due to poverty. They may even disappear from the area. They just don't care: prison may mean a good rest... but you never know; there is always the chance that they will actually pay in full, so good luck to you!

You may derive some satisfaction from the fact that, having alerted the local populace, other innocents will be saved from a similar experience, so there really are positive results from this sorry affair, even if you are not recompensed.

Not the least of these positive results is that you will not make the same mistake again. Now you can see how valuable meticulous *advance* checks can be. There are many ways and degrees of winning!

Keep complaining EFFECTIVELY.

CHAPTER 9

Is this seat taken?

CHAPTER 9

We now come to:

GOODS

It is worthwhile to clarify the difference between *goods* and *services*. Services are intangible, something you cannot physically touch.

Goods are tangible, ranging from a pork pie at one end of the scale to an expensive armchair at the other. The only thing they have in common is that you can touch them.

Of course this is obvious to *you*, dear reader, but I never cease to be amazed at the number of people who, when asked, are simply unable to tell the difference.

For our purposes, let us examine the humble pork pie. *This* one is a mouldy pork pie. Whilst shopping in your supermarket you buy a package of two pies. They appear, when viewed through the transparent packaging, to be in perfect condition, but, just in case, you check the 'sell by' date. Your potential purchase is within the limit, so into the trolley it goes.

Having selected a number of other items, you are about to leave the store when a 'bargain offer' of electric kettles at five pounds each catches your eye. At that price you cannot resist the offer, so you include the item with your other purchases, pay in cash and retain the receipt.

Arriving home, you remove the pork pies from their packaging, cut them into slices and prepare them for a snack. You are dismayed to discover that, whereas one is of normal appearance, the other contains what seems to be mouldy meat filling.

Next you half fill the kettle with water, plug it into the electric socket and – yes, you have guessed already! – it fails to heat up.

RULE 8

Wherever possible examine a product you intend to buy for faults or defects BEFORE you pay for it.

Of course, you are not going to open up the package of pork pies and take a bite out of each first, just to make sure they are all right; much as I like the idea of customers in a supermarket merrily munching on their intended purchases before paying at the check-out! It is perhaps debateable whether you would get away with it provided you paid for all the satisfactory items on the spot, or whether you might be referred to a psychiatrist. In any event, why not give it a whirl? It would certainly brighten up the day for a lot of people!

In any case, of course, you can take the offending pie, together with the 'good' one, the packaging *and* a copy of the receipt back to the store and expect to obtain a refund.

I emphasise a *copy* of the receipt in this case: remember the kettle is included in the same receipt and you will not want to hand over the original, as you might be expected to do; it may be your intention to complain about each of the two items i.e. pork pie and kettle, in separate ways.

Incidentally, if, dear reader, you feel that pork pies are too trivial a matter to complain about and not to be compared with, for example, a mouldy wedding cake with all the ramifications easily imagined, just hold your horses.

I confess that it was I who complained about this particular pork pie, a thing of slight importance in the great scheme of things, seemingly, but of considerable importance when what is involved amounts to a principle; any item you purchase should be suitable and appropriate to fulfil the purpose for which it is intended. Quite apart from the fact that millions of pork pies are consumed annually and only one in a thousand turns out to be 'unfit for intended use', that represents a fair number of unhappy customers as well as a great deal of misspent cash.

So, sticking for the moment to our lowly pork pies, I *prefer* to complain to the store's marketing manager at head office level if the pies are the store's 'own brand' product.

Now note the content of this sample letter:

RECORDED DELIVERY

Your name and address

Mr/Mrs (name), Marketing Manager
Store Group head office address

Dear -----

    On the (date) I purchased two pork pies in one unit packaging from your branch store at (address). One was perfectly edible but the other contained what appeared to be mouldy meat.

    Rather than return the item to your branch for a refund, I choose to advise you directly, enclosing herewith a very small sample of the offending meat in sealed cling-film, together with a copy of the receipt of purchase.

    Please note that I have sent a copy of this letter to your head of quality control for analysis similarly enclosing a tiny sample for this department's analysis.

    I trust you will arrange appropriate recompense in due course and I hope that I have been of assistance in bringing this matter to your attention.

    Yours sincerely,
    (signature)

ANALYSIS OF THIS LETTER

a) Had the complaint been made by returning the pies, packaging and receipt to the store, a full refund would doubtless have been made on the spot.

b) It is also likely that a cursory entry would have been made in the branch complaints book, signed by you and possibly even asking for your phone number. *Never* give your phone number. The matter would have ended with the refund…?

c) Should b) above have occurred, no further action would have been taken, simply because the amount of additional paperwork and effort generated at local level would (multiplied by x number of all other complaints) clog up management and staff time to an unacceptable extent.

   I have actually checked that this is indeed the view of at least one branch manager (who added, incidentally: 'Head Office will deny this'!) Mmmm …

d) …. on the other hand, the group's quality control department is keenly interested in such instances; quality control is their raison d'être.

e) Moreover, the marketing manager seemed very pleased to hear from an actual customer with a valid complaint; possibly for reasons of his own. Perhaps he may well have preferred me *not* to have alerted quality control at the same time …?

f) In such hierarchies as these, the *marketing manager* is most often potential board management material; with all the nuances this implies.

Please note that although I am not particularly suspicious by nature, such situations as I have outlined above do exist, to my certain knowledge.

You may now smile a little at the outcome – three vouchers amounting to a princely sum were received, to be spent on any items in the store!

Now, to exercise *your* method of analysis, consider this:

Suppose these pork pies had been produced and packaged by a BRAND NAME. Would we complain differently, and if so, why?

NO. We would go through the same procedure (sigh of relief).

There is, however, a significant difference in that an independently owned Branded Product supplier is going to be ultra careful in checking and analysing the faulty product.

This is not to say that the 'own brand' store product quality control department is not going to be careful; it *is* to say that the outside supplier's product, quite apart from being supplied to supermarkets may well be available at a vast number of other outlets both nationally and even *globally*.

The scrutiny of potentially faulty products undertaken by these corporations is of the most intense, thorough and detailed kind, thank goodness! Without being unduly cynical, it should be said that this is very much to their commercial advantage, although some would perhaps have us believe that their assiduous scrutiny is solely for the customer's protection.

Special Note

It should have become apparent by now that, in keeping pace with an ever-increasing diversity of complaints exposed for your scrutiny and analysis and dealt with effectively, our approach to these differing complaints requires refinement and modification.

A prime example in the instance we have just examined is the decision to complain to the marketing manager as well as to the quality control monitor and not – as is usually the case – directly to the Chairman or Chief Executive Officer, with copies to the other two.

The latter are the 'prime movers' and decision makers and in this particular instance undoubtedly have the necessary authority and interest in solving the problem.

Should we be dissatisfied with their response (or lack of it) we would refer to their superiors.

Using *your own judgement* in the application of our rules and techniques is of the essence!

We will now consider the case of the electric kettle bought from the supermarket.

It is reasonable to assume that most people do not have the time to unpack a kettle after purchase whilst still on the premises. However, it would be interesting to discover what would happen if a customer did in fact ask to test electrical goods in store immediately after actually making a purchase.

Seeking an answer to this contingency, I contacted nine different supermarkets and enquired what the store's response would be if asked to test an electrical appliance immediately after paying for it.

Of the nine stores questioned, two said they saw no objection to the idea. Four agreed that although it might present a problem, they would try to sort it out with the customer but one of the four added that '… it could be a real problem if everyone demanded to check that the appliance was in working order!'

Three refused to answer the question, claiming that it involved 'sensitive' information. Honestly!

Readers, don't be surprised. You're right: 'Call Centre Response'!

In every case but one, I was put through to a call centre and had to wait a long time (up to 8 minutes delay) before I received any sort of answer.

It was often necessary to make two or more telephone calls to obtain even a non-committal response. Good job I wasn't attempting to make a complaint.

Of the two stores who 'couldn't see a problem', one – just one – actually said the situation had already arisen, could not find a suitable socket to test the item on the sales floor but were eventually able to use the manager's office.

For the latter information I have to thank a young sales assistant. It was she who actually first answered my telephone enquiry, adding that 'it caused quite a stir and we all had a good laugh about it'. For obvious reasons I cannot divulge the young lady's name or indeed that of the supermarket but would like, all the same, to put my thanks on record.

And now, dear reader, after logging up the cost of all those telephone calls (£8.30) what do you make of the situation?

It would appear that those hardy souls with shopping time to spare and the required bloody-mindedness and persistence might, at best, find a store which *possibly* could find somewhere to test their kettle. Those who have not yet read this book will carry on buying kettles, testing them when they get home and if they fail to work, returning no doubt to the store with their problem.

Remember the procedure for the pork pies? Our kettle is a branded item, sold on to the supermarket, so follow exactly the same procedure. Under no circumstances take up your complaint with the store where you bought the kettle.

This, I feel, is an appropriate moment to raise a *general* issue concerning complaints:-

Only complain when after careful consideration you honestly feel that the complaint is genuinely justified.

For your own sake, *don't* take up complaining as a hobby: there are undoubtedly many out there who cannot wait to find something (or anything) to complain about. It goes without saying that you, dear reader, are not one of that number!

We are all acquainted with the sort of angry person we cross the road to avoid ... on the other hand; for all you honest readers with a genuine cause for complaint there is often an additional benefit to be obtained from implementing the procedures illustrated in this book: you will find that some of the companies to whom you feel obliged to complain will express their genuine thanks and appreciation not only by letter, but by offering you cash vouchers or the like well in excess of the value of the items involved. Sometimes they will find remarkably innovative ways of expressing their appreciation of your helpful criticism. It is most gratifying to be thanked for complaining – effectively, of course.

I turn now to another sample case, concluding this section under our 'Goods' heading.

The case I am about to outline is a truly extraordinary one, illustrating an interesting style of Complaining Effectively. I have verified the facts of this rather odd specimen and am satisfied that we are dealing with fact not fiction. It is included here for your scrutiny, analysis and evaluation of the appropriate method of complaint to be adopted.

The case concerns a gentlemen who visited a well-known and well-established firm in private ownership specialising in good quality brand-new furniture.

The firm was holding a closing-down sale. The gentleman noticed in the shop window a new armchair offered at a bargain price. What attracted him most to the armchair was the fact that it was precisely the shade of colour he was looking for: it perfectly matched the decor of his room.

A salesman explained that this was a 'one off' bargain; he could not guarantee that it would remain unsold until the following weekend.

The prospective purchaser made an on-the-spot decision to buy the armchair and offered to pay cash, with the proviso that the shop would guarantee to deliver it on the date and at the time he specified.

The owner of the shop was called over to handle the transaction and confirm the delivery details. The bargain price was paid in cash against a receipt on headed notepaper on which the delivery details were specified precisely, with the proprietor's signature appended to authenticate the transaction. There appeared no room for error or misunderstanding.

As he outlined the situation to me; the purchaser, realising that he would not be at home until very late in the evening on the agreed delivery date, explained to the shop owner that his wife would take delivery. All this was cordially agreed.

The armchair was duly delivered and accepted on the date and at the time agreed by the purchaser's wife.

There was only one problem: when the husband arrived home, the first thing he noticed was that the armchair, though in all other respects exactly what he had ordered was in a *different colour*.

He complained by telephone the following morning but although the proprietor sympathised, he informed his by now dissatisfied customer that the salesman had, regrettably, sold the chair in the shop window to someone else. The one delivered by the shop was the only other one left…

Our man wanted the name and address of the manufacturer in order to lodge a complaint. This was provided by the proprietor who pointed out, however, that the chair had been made in Sweden and in any case the shop had already closed its account with the supplier. The purchaser then asked for a full refund to be made immediately. He received an unequivocal refusal.

It is at this point that the purchaser decided upon an interesting ploy to gain his refund.

The following morning, he and a neighbour loaded the chair into his estate car, drove to the shop just before it opened, unloaded the armchair on to the pavement outside and while the neighbour parked the vehicle nearby, sat calmly down in the armchair to await developments.

Meanwhile, he informed all passers-by that the shop had *taken his money under false pretences*.

When the shop opened and the owner saw what was happening he at once handed over the money in full; explaining that it had 'all been a misunderstanding'.

This, dear reader, is scarcely a course of action I would recommend but it is without doubt another method of Complaining Effectively.

We all, so they say, live and learn. The situation could, of course, have gone disastrously wrong, attracting police involvement, charges of harassment, etc.

Nevertheless, it worked.

CHAPTER 10

Bully Boys

CHAPTER 10

This chapter is designed, in a sense, for you, dear reader, to arrive at a self-assessment.

I shall present you with a situation which, at first glance, may seem to have only a vague connection with the mastering of those techniques and disciplines required in Complaining Effectively.

Allow me to explain what I would like you to do to help yourself in the overall task of complaining with maximum impact.

a) Read the following factual case history first.

b) Having realised in the course of the narrative that the complainant is rescued from what appears initially to be an inexorable downward spiral to eventual defeat and is then rescued from the consequences by sheer good fortune, *put yourself in his shoes*; immerse yourself in his feelings and his plight. *Become that person*, as it were, from the very onset of his troubles, look at what sort of chap he seems to be, then ask yourself:

c) How would I have reacted in this situation, armed with the calm, disciplined approach recommended in this book?

d) Would my newly learned skills have been sufficient to achieve a successful outcome?

e) How many different ways can I think of to solve the problem?

f) Which solution option shall I adopt?

g) Would this positive solution I choose enable me to solve the problem soonest?

h) Will a speedy solution in itself ensure that the problem will not recur in the future?

i) Answer honestly the question: Had I been in this fellow's *frame of mind* from day *one*, could I have halted and contained – or indeed, altered – my attitude in terms of desperate feelings of fear, isolation, loneliness and sheer panic which so clearly coloured his ability to examine the problem and decide on a subsequent course of action in an objective and calm manner?

j) Write down your own analysis of the problem and in so doing incorporate answers to the above questions.

Incidentally, if you come up with alternative – (better?) – solutions when considering my recommended actions, don't be surprised. I shall be truly delighted.

Here, then, are the facts:

The Terrorising of Julian (not, of course, his real name)

Julian was in his mid-fifties, slight of build and inoffensive of manner, a successful technical specialist in the industrial sector. This sector being subject to massive change in manufacturing methods meant that his special skills were becoming out-dated. In addition, huge numbers of employees were being made redundant. He was one of these. Nevertheless he still felt confident that there was a niche somewhere in the newly re-formed industry for him and his special skills. He determined to set up a small freelance outfit of his own. He did so. It failed and he was left literally penniless.

The man lost everything. He was homeless. Being a single man and a loner he was ... alone!

No family, nothing!

He applied for – and obtained – state benefit and was most fortunate to be allocated a tiny flat on a run-down housing estate, operated by a Housing Association.

He moved into his new home and on the very first day of his occupancy, *it started*.

Unbeknown to him at the time, his next-door neighbour was a thorough bully. To make matters worse, he was sandwiched in between two bullies as it turned out that his other neighbour was one of the first man's henchmen.

The first week encompassed the shouting of pointed abuse and innuendo outside his front door, unsigned threatening notes thrust through his letterbox and dog faeces smeared on his bedroom window. Gradually, the imaginative harassment increased in scope and frequency.

Appeals to the Police resulted in a solitary visit both to the bully, his acolyte and Julian himself.

The bully and his acolyte backed each other up in denying everything.

Julian was told by the Police to keep a log of the 'alleged' offences, as they described them. They also told him to advise the Housing Association's Tenant Relations Department who *eventually* sent a warning letter to the bully himself who denied any responsibility for the incidents referred to, backed up his 'friend'.

Counter-allegations of provocative, aggressive and threatening behaviour were made against Julian.

Again, he was asked by the Housing Association to log all the events he 'alleged' to have taken place and keep the Police informed. Weeks became months, but no positive moves were made to follow up and solve the problem, let alone quickly. Julian complied with the Police and Housing Association's suggestions and logged each incident: date, time and nature of the actions perpetrated by his tormentors. For Julian, long gone were the days of calm, rational thinking on the problem. He was reduced to a level of basic instinct.

His attempts to discuss the matter and solve any problems with the bully or his pal were rebuffed. He had tried this at the beginning and was laughed at by both. Worse still, he took to his bed, only answered the door when he looked out through his spy-hole to establish a visitor's identity. He scurried to and from his local shop for essential provisions. He was quite simply reduced to irrational animal-like behaviour.

Life had become, for Julian, a torment; a living hell.

Then a glimmer of hope appeared. Purely by chance, it seemed, a newly appointed local Police 'beat bobby' knocked on his door. Julian learned subsequently that people serving in his local shop had mentioned that one of their customers was behaving in a peculiar manner and seemed to have changed recently. This had prompted the officer's visit.

Julian admitted him into his home, described his plight and found, as he later described it to me, that the officer *'really listened'*. As you will now realise, it was only a long time after these events that Julian told me his sad story.

To continue:

Astonishingly, to Julian, the constable took *immediate* action. Julian was provided (discreetly) by the officer with a live video-audio recording unit, installed to record all sights and sounds immediately outside the flat by means of two tiny cameras and microphones sited within his home. These were in operation twenty-four hours a day, seven days a week.

Within two weeks, the Police had sufficient evidence to invite the bully and his partner in crime to the Police Station where they were taken to the interview room, cautioned and then confronted on a video screen with an edited replay of the surveillance evidence. This showed incident upon incident with sound accompaniment, of the harassment and distress they had inflicted on Julian.

They were then invited to comment. Incredibly, they tried to shrug off these appalling scenes with an explanation that it was all a joke!

Of course they were immediately formally charged with harassment and subsequently officially warned; Julian was provided with a formal letter by the area Police Commander guaranteeing him protection which he carries to this day.

It may be of interest to you that all of the above occurred some eleven years ago. Julian is now content, has become a success in a new-found latter day career. The bullies have never dared to approach or communicate with him since. Even more to the point, they realise that should he ever need to report them for harassment again – *at any time in the future* – by the terms of the formal warning served upon them they will be liable to immediate arrest and sent to prison.

MY Analysis.

I separate the analysis into two distinct areas:

1) My tactics if I were in Julian's position at the very beginning of the tenancy.

2) My tactics if I were asked to advise him mid-way through his ordeal.

Firstly:

At the very onset, on the initial indication of antagonism shown by the main bully I would *appear* to him to be hurt by his attitude and at whatever cost to my feelings would ensure I approached him calmly, with a smile. I would then ask him if I had unwittingly offended him.

Option 1

I suggest that his response is hardly likely to be anything but dismissive and possibly evasive. He might refuse to discuss the matter.

Option 2

He could agree to discuss the matter, pretending willingness to be reasonable, then during the discussion laugh about it whilst in attitude and body signals attempt to establish his dominance and superiority from the beginning.

Whichever option he adopts, alarm bells immediately start ringing in my mind.

NOTE

A *notional Option 3* is that I could attempt to calm him down, discuss matters rationally and achieve a reasonable, objective, satisfactory conclusion. In my view and experience such an approach in this case is 'pie in the sky' hope. *We*, readers, have of a certainty met such 'creatures' in our lives. This evaluation is accurate, as subsequent events illustrate.

TACTICS

In both options 1 and 2 it is clear in my mind that immediate and decisive action must be implemented against him. Remember our axiom – seize and hold on to an advantage at the earliest opportunity. Control the situation before it controls you. My prompt action takes the form of a Recorded Delivery letter (standard practice by now) as follows:

RECORDED DELIVERY

>Yours name and address
>Date

(Name) Chairman of the Housing Association
Address

COMPLAINT

Dear ---

I moved into the above premises on (date).

On the (date) my neighbour Mr --- of (address) perpetrated harassment against me. (Give precise details of occurrence/s).

I approached him on (date), being the following day, to ask if I had offended him in any way and if so could we please discuss the matter calmly and reasonably.

His response was (describe his precise response, not forgetting to include attitude and body signals).

It is of course my wish that Mr --- and I should live as good neighbours in harmony, without, of course, intruding unduly into each other's privacy.

I will continue to maintain a peaceful attitude towards Mr --- and trust that the incident was a one-off occurrence.

However, as a sensible precaution as well as courtesy to yourself I think it wise to advise you of this problem and will keep you informed of any further incidents of harassment should they unfortunately occur.

Finally I must add that I feel it prudent to keep a careful detailed log of any future incidents.

Please note that I have sent copies of this letter to those persons/organisations listed below.

Yours sincerely,
(signature)

c.c. Director of Social Services (name)
Clerk to the Council (name), Town Council
Tenant Liaison Manager (name), Housing Association
Duty Officer (name and rank), Local Police

NOTE

You may think that sending all these copies of the letter to the Chairman is massively 'over the top'. I agree, but remember, an all-out pre-emptive attack is needed to nip the bullies' antics in the bud.

Note also that the master bully is kept totally in the dark about my action, both now and in the future.

Of course, no harm is done if it all turns out to be storm in a teacup … *We* know, reader, that this is not the case, don't we?

We allow two more weeks of hell to elapse, meanwhile keeping our own counsel, in silence.

Further incidents of harassment take place during these two weeks. We log each one of them and set it out in written form as promised to the Chairman of the Housing Association.

Our letter will certainly be acknowledged and we *may expect* (doubtfully) to receive copies of any letters sent to the bullies by the authorities listed, but these will be, at least at the start of the affair, rather weak letters about tenants' behaviour: Housing Associations have a strict procedure in such matters, and short of there being serial killers on the rampage, they will trundle out the same old 'guff'.

We are having none of that, dear reader!

At the end of the two week period, out goes our next letter to the Chairman of the Housing Association:

RECORDED DELIVERY

Dear Sir,

I refer to my letter dated (---) concerning my complaint as specified therein.

In the matter of harassment and the possible increase in frequency thereof, you will be aware from all the letters I have sent you (in particular a copy of each sent to your Liaison Manager) that action on the part of the Housing Association consists of standard letters of warning.

I admit to no surprise as your organisation is clearly following a standard procedure. This is, of course, very little help to me as the recipient of these outrages. My health has deteriorated dramatically and I will be sending you my doctor's letter confirming this.

I am fully aware that it *is* in your power to take immediate action to resolve this problem.

Please accept, therefore, as formal notice, that I am sending today by Recorded Delivery a copy of this letter to all the parties listed in my earlier letter to you, together with a covering letter to each of them and enclosing a copy of the fully comprehensive log of each individual incident.

I am sorry to have to resort to these measures but nevertheless I am prepared to allow a further *seven days only* as from the date of this letter to receive formal notice in writing from you proving that you have established proceedings against the perpetrators of this harassment.

Naturally you will understand that my health is of prime concern to me.

Failure to receive such written assurance will leave me just one recourse: to act as I see fit.

Yours sincerely,
(signature)

c.c.   As before

Should the local Police fail at this stage to respond, the next step will be a letter to the Chief Constable.

I leave it to you to consider what, if necessary, I write to the Chief Constable but bear in mind that letters (with all supporting relevant correspondence) would go additionally to the Independent Police Complaints Commission (IPCC), the Press, the local MP, the representative of the European Parliament – in other words, to Uncle Tom Cobley and all. THIS IS NOT A GAME!

Reader, we do not mess about! In particular, we make certain we do all this after seven days. With certainty, I think we can look forward to a speedy resolution of the problem.

The lesson to be learnt here by all those involved is that *we never ease up on the pressure we apply*. In addition, *we act promptly*.

We mean it. We *complain effectively*.

TACTICS: ANALYSIS

You will recall that I mentioned earlier, under 'tactics' (2):

'If I were to advise Julian mid-way through his predicament...'

My answer is of course obvious (see earlier chapters on coming in to help when the complainant is half-way through his/her – untrained – attempts at complaining). I would obtain authorisation to act on the complainant's behalf then action the complaints process with *our* discipline in place, gaining a quick, planned, positive outcome.

You will be fully conversant with our methods by now, dear reader, and may permit yourself a knowing smile.

OVER TO YOU

Well, reader, how did you get on with your own analysis? I am quite sure you solved the problem, if not effortlessly, then at least with all your new-found armour in place, *positively*. Well done!

There are a few loose ends which I need to sort out for you.

a) *Police Surveillance Equipment*

In the example given above, it should be noted that if such equipment is not readily available for use, you are entitled, having stated your case, to ask for it to be supplied. The Police have only limited supplies of equipment and limited time but at least you will receive a sympathetic hearing for your application. It will be judged on its merits – fairly.

You can of course hire such equipment privately. If your health is suffering severely, you will find it a sensible, worthwhile option.

Should *you* ever have the need to hire surveillance equipment *privately* for whatever reason I recommend that before doing so, you consult with the Police FIRST!

b)   Private unauthorised surveillance may be either illegal/not legally admissible in court – or both.

The case I quote above illustrates clearly that the Police installed and removed their own equipment.

There are mediation services available where such disputes can (we hope) be resolved. My knowledge and experience of bullies in general lead me to the sad conclusion that the very last thing such people want is to face up to their behaviour and mend their ways. If you wish, by all means give such services an opportunity – my worry is that precious time elapses whilst *a victim continues to suffer*.

c)   … a curious question, reader?

Would you have simply punched the fellow, in the hope that would solve the problem?

Do remember this could result in a charge of assault. Your well-aimed punch would certainly not improve your case. In addition, the Police could then take the view that this matter was a 'private dispute between neighbours', with all that that implies.

CHAPTER 11

The End of the Line

CHAPTER 11

As we draw to a conclusion…

It is my earnest, heart-felt wish that I have been the source of some help, encouragement and hope in whatever circumstances that may have prompted you to pick up this book in the first place.

One of the most compelling reasons prompting me to set down in print the foregoing guidelines is the personal knowledge and awareness of the *loneliness* implicit in Complaining Effectively.

When you feel that an injustice is being done, it can be hard to decide which course of action to take. Your mind can become overwhelmed and confused when faced with a problem presenting many options for action.

One of the fears – and there are many – that come to mind is that putting pen to paper is in itself an alarming prospect. Simply having to write a letter – even when you know what you want to say, can cause *deeper* worries: what if I make spelling mistakes? I must remember to be calm … I must be sure to include …

You may not have written a letter for years; perhaps you have never had to write a letter and imagine yourself incapable of doing so.

Nevertheless, you have persevered: you have read this book. With patience, you *can* do it. You may wish to revise and correct your letter a number of times – so many – that the very thought freezes you into inaction.

Another major concern I have for you, is that before you even *begin* to do anything, lack of confidence, low personal esteem, the stress brought on by the problem you face – any or all of these things can stop you in your tracks *before you even begin* to tackle the problem.

I genuinely and wholeheartedly empathise with you, dear reader. I too have suffered just such fears as *you* are now experiencing. We both know that it is frequently useless to say to yourself 'come on, you can do it!' When you get into such a state, nothing seems to help.

The *only* way I know to overcome such feelings is to exhaust myself to the limit with my concerns then say to myself: That's it! To hell with it, I don't care any more (even though in your heart of hearts you do), I will sit down, put the first letter together and post it.

You are now in for a surprise. That first positive letter will do wonders for your self confidence. Suddenly you are free! The shackles are off, so now go ahead and *win*. The loneliness, worry and enervating stress will ebb away with every step you take. Calm, considered, thoughtful ACTION will disperse all the loneliness and frustration.

Now go to it, knowing that I am behind you every step of the way.

Good luck has nothing to do with it – you are in charge. Do remember (and I say this with the gentlest of smiles) amid the euphoria of winning, that you are now equipped with the knowledge to help *someone else* when their need arises.

One day soon, we shall all be COMPLAINING EFFECTIVELY.

GUIDE

To locate each RULE

No. 1	See page 14
No. 2	See page 15
No. 3	See page 17
No. 4	See page 19
No. 5	See page 28
No. 6	See page 69
No. 7	See page 76
No. 8	See page 122